Book #1 in the "Created for" Series

CREATED *for* SIGNIFICANCE

Discovering Our Human Core Longings,
Who Defines Us, and
How We Reverse Identity Theft

Robert B. Shaw, Jr.

Foreword by Dr. Tim Clinton

Copyright © 2013 Dr. Robert B. Shaw, Jr.

All rights reserved. No part of this book may be used or reproduced by any means, graphic, electronic, or mechanical, including photocopying, recording, taping or by any information storage retrieval system without the written permission of the publisher except in the case of brief quotations embodied in critical articles and reviews.

WestBow Press books may be ordered through booksellers or by contacting:

WestBow Press
A Division of Thomas Nelson
1663 Liberty Drive
Bloomington, IN 47403
www.westbowpress.com
1-(866) 928-1240

Because of the dynamic nature of the Internet, any web addresses or links contained in this book may have changed since publication and may no longer be valid. The views expressed in this work are solely those of the author and do not necessarily reflect the views of the publisher, and the publisher hereby disclaims any responsibility for them.

Any people depicted in stock imagery provided by Thinkstock are models, and such images are being used for illustrative purposes only.

Certain stock imagery © Thinkstock.

ISBN: 978-1-4497-9473-6 (sc)
ISBN: 978-1-4497-9474-3 (hc)
ISBN: 978-1-4497-9472-9 (e)

Library of Congress Control Number: 2013908385

Printed in the United States of America.

Unless otherwise noted, all scriptural references are from the New American Standard Version of the Holy Bible, Revised Edition, Copyright 1999 by the Zondervan Corporation.

WestBow Press rev. date: 09/26/2013

Acknowledgements

I want to thank Ms. Donna Makofsky and Ms. Michele Worley for providing input and suggestions as faithful proofreaders.

I want to thank Bishop Dr. Mark Chironna for his faithful and constant encouragement. But mostly for his friendship.

I want to thank Pastor David Longobardo for continuing to encourage me in my pursuit of ministry to aid hurting people and for his faithfulness in ministering to my family for many years.

I want to thank my Senior Pastor, Adrian Starks, for his ministry, faithfulness, and support of what God is doing in my life.

I want to thank Dr. Tim Clinton for his affirmation and for providing me opportunities to continue fulfilling my purpose with significance.

I want to bless my five wonderful children Aaron, Kenneth, April, Jeremy, and Bonnie for being the arrows in my quiver. There is no one I enjoy being around more than my family.

I want to thank my dear and beautiful wife, Lorinda, for her love, commitment, and encouragement as we journey together through peaks and valleys. I cannot put into words what you mean to me.

Finally, I want to thank my Lord Jesus, for my salvation, His favor on my life, and for all He has revealed to me. Still, I know I haven't seen anything yet.

Contents

Foreword	Dr. Tim Clinton	ix
Introduction		xiii
Chapter 1	The Identity Theft Problem	1
Chapter 2	Core Longings	17
Chapter 3	What's in a Name?	32
Chapter 4	It All Starts with How We View God	41
Chapter 5	Wounds Often Redefine Who We Are	54
Chapter 6	A New Name Brings a New Destiny	72
Chapter 7	A Balanced Approach to the Self	90
Chapter 8	Some Names We Call Ourselves	103
Chapter 9	The Truth Will Set You Free—And Change Your Name	117
References		137

Foreword

Consider a moment in time when you felt valued. Treasured. Noticed. For most of us, that memory ties in somehow with performance and the approval of others. The crowds cheering wildly as you got the "walk-off" hit and won the game. Your parents beaming with pride as you took first place in the beauty pageant. Your coach's "atta boy" as you saved the tournament with your last-second basketball shot. Teachers' accolades as you took the podium to address your classmates as valedictorian. The applause of your co-workers as you walked forward to receive an award.

In today's world, we often equate performance with significance. However, this mindset can suck us into a crazy cycle—driven to do anything and everything to win the approval of others. Ever been there? The problem is, it never lasts. You're only as good as your last hit or your last dance.

Plagued with these insecurities, many people then turn to drugs and sex or workaholism and ministry—anything to silence the lies and numb their pain. When we mistake performance for significance, we build our lives on a fragile foundation. One slip, one mistake…and our identity breaks apart. Basing our self-worth on others' approval is much like Jesus' parable of the house built on sand: "The moment the torrent struck that house, it collapsed and its destruction was complete" (Luke 6:49). When we rely on others for our identity, we end up living in fear of failure, constantly trying to do more and be more to try to ward off the overwhelming insecurities we feel.

What's interesting, however, is that this deep "longing for significance" is God-given. We long to be known and loved for who we are precisely because God made us that way. Our true identity is to be rooted and anchored in Him—how He sees us and values us—not in what we do or what others think of us. Jesus said, "You will know the truth, and the truth will set you free" (John 8:39). In this book, Dr. Bob Shaw addresses significance and introduces other core longings of the heart that are critical to acknowledge in order to move from bondage to freedom in our lives.

In Psalm 46:10, the Psalmist tells us to be still…to cease striving. Our Heavenly Father beckons us to know that He is God. Discovering our God-given identity starts with knowing God. As we seek Him, we also come to see ourselves as His unique and treasured creation, redeemed by Jesus Christ and set apart to serve Him! The knowledge that we are celebrated, cherished, and valued by the Creator of the universe will change us from the inside out. One of my favorite passages is in Acts 17:28: "For in Him we live and move and have our being." Nothing less than this glorious truth can ever bring us to true, unwavering significance.

I pray that as Dr. Bob Shaw explores the roots of our God-given identity, you'll learn how your sense of self was shattered by sin, but redeemed through Jesus Christ—and what that means for you today. Along the way, you'll read about biblical characters who were broken and flawed just like us, yet came to know true significance in their lives. Explore these pages and discover your true identity as a cherished son or daughter of your loving Heavenly Father. He loves you with an everlasting love, and through Him, you can find lasting significance, a place to ground your heart and life.

Dr. Tim Clinton, LPC; LMFT
President, American Association of Christian Counselors (AACC)
Forest, VA
Executive Director, Center for Counseling and Family Studies and Professor of Counseling and Pastoral Care
Liberty University
Lynchburg, VA

Introduction

When I was growing up in the inner city and then in the suburban environments of New Jersey, the neighborhood kids had an expression: "Sticks and stones may break my bones but names will never hurt me!" I am sure many of you heard or recited a similar ditty. A child may hear someone call him or her names like "jerk," "dork," "unwanted," "failure," "ugly," or "spaz," and the above expression would be a noble attempt to deflect such names and criticisms. While this statement was intended to repel hurtful names and labels, the reality is, names did hurt—and often stuck! They often hurt more than sticks and stones. It is such names and labels that can have a damaging, even devastating effect on a youngster. Names and labels are often carried into adulthood as descriptions that stick, and we tend to believe them for the rest of our lives. We often mistakenly base our significance on such names. The names and beliefs regarding our significance translate into behaviors, leading the individual into either positive or negative consequences and positive or negative relationships.

Over the years I have spoken to several physicians who have acknowledged that my job as a minister or counselor was often more difficult than their profession. They would reason that they could see most of the wounds and ailments in people, through the naked eye, X-rays, MRI's, and other technology. These tools helped identify the broken bones or biological internal wounds caused by physical "sticks and stones," so to speak. Such knowledge tremendously helped these professionals in creating treatment plans for their hurting clients.

Wounds to the soul, however, are not as readily seen and can be difficult to pinpoint. Yet they can have an equal if not greater effect upon an individual's life and relationships. Words and harmful actions from significant people in our lives, especially when we are young, can produce labels, outlooks on life, self-worth, and abilities that can impact meaningful relationships. These names, labels, and self-beliefs can hinder the *core longings* that exist in every human being. That is, of course, until such names are challenged and changed by the truth of who we really are and how we are really valued.

Thanks to the teachings of Dr. Anne Halley, through Ashland Theological Seminary, and the many individuals and couples I have had the privilege of ministering to, I have come to understand and appreciate that we as human beings are all wired with the same core longings and the need for them to be met. Before the sinful fall of Adam and Eve in Genesis 3, these deep human desires were met directly by God Himself. After Adam and Eve sinned, relationship with God was broken. Man and woman mistakenly believed they were then left to meet their own longings and desires through their own efforts.

Ever since the rebellion in Eden, people have been making that same mistake. Broken relationship with God leads to selfish and evil ways of meeting these longings. Such pursuits alter our identity and change who we are, which in turn further ruins relationships. I see the brokenness in people almost every day now as they try to meet their deep longings. I witness wounded people's attempts to recover from being used and abused by others, who themselves were using hateful and evil ways of obtaining that which they felt they needed.

This book will introduce what I believe are the six core longings in every human being. Then I will focus on the core longing of significance as the main subject of this book, with future titles to present the other five core longings. This series will be titled the "Created For" series:

Created for Significance
Created for Covering (Safety)
Created for Purpose
Created for Belonging
Created for Understanding
Created for Love

Significance means the *importance* or the *meaning* of something or someone. In other words, significance is related to our identity. Such truth is not easy to come by in our overly critical, name-calling, cynical society. To hear affirmations and receive what American psychologist Carl Rogers (1902-87) calls "positive regard" is something everyone needs but is often scarce. Significant people in our lives often have much impact and power to render either curses or blessings. However, in this competitive and disrespectful environment in which we live, put downs are more prominent than praises. As a result, our identities and the meaningfulness of our lives become casualties to the put downs, abuses, and materialistic worldviews.

But there is good news! God sees us so differently than how others see us. God also sees us differently than we see ourselves. It is often difficult to change the labels we believe to be true to the way God has defined and designed us to be. Somewhere along the way, someone or something has altered or destroyed the significance of our lives. Names that have become who we are, what we do or don't do, and how we see ourselves as we relate to our world somehow does not meet the desire to feel significant. Many of us have experienced disappointing and traumatically hurtful situations that have robbed our identity. Many of us have "flipped our own labels" through negative and inaccurate self-talk. God has a way of letting us know He values us in such a way that these names and labels can be reversed. The truth is, we are significant to Him!

It is critical that we begin to allow God to define us. It is also critical for us to see God accurately for who He is as well. Dr. Joseph M. Stowell writes, "If you live with a distorted view of someone, you will inevitably pass it on to others" (Stowell, 2003).

If we live with a distorted view of God, we express that to others in our life. Living with a distorted view of ourselves will cause us to present ourselves a certain way to others. Unless we see ourselves as God sees us, we may be forever in bondage to the names and labels that were once given to us as a child. We have often given other individuals the power to define who we are. This occurs in many ways: through spoken words, traumatic events, hurtful events, abuse, and neglect, just to name a few. In order for inner healing and right understanding of who we are to transpire, a person needs to allow God to have His say and touch our damaged and wounded spirit.

There are basically three ways to view God and man. One is to have a good opinion of self and a bad opinion of God. This is essentially humanism. This view asserts that self-discovery lies within, and God is not necessary in the process. Man can experience self-actualization on his own, and as a result can discover who he or she is and become good. However, leaving God out is deadly.

The second way is to have a bad opinion of self and a good opinion of God. Many Christians fall into this category. We are indeed born into sin and operate through a fallen, sinful nature. We may have accepted Jesus Christ's finished work for us on the cross and been redeemed, yet we may have trouble believing God actually loves us and desires good things for our lives while we are still on Earth. We may believe God is good and loving, but we somehow are still trying to earn more of His love. Some people I have come across have even stated that God cannot possibly love them because of who they are and what they did in the past.

Then there is a third way to view God and man. That is to have a good opinion of self and a good opinion of God. A good opinion of self does not have to be one of self-centeredness. A good opinion of self should include the awareness and confession that we are indeed sinners, but that God loved us so much, "that while we were yet sinners, Christ died for us" (Rom. 5:8). While we were wretched without God, *He saw* us as significant and worthy of saving and made a way for restoration of our standing in Him. A good opinion of self may not occur until after we accept Christ and see how much He loves and cherishes us. Our daily need for a Savior keeps things in a healthy perspective. A good God created man and woman and called His creation "very good" (Gen. 1:28). He loved humans even when we fell into sin and rebellion, and made provision for us to be seen as good again, through the finished work of Christ. A good God has made human beings good again, but only by His grace and provision. As a result, individuals have been saved and empowered to fulfill their destiny and enjoy God's presence, love, healing, and gifts to live a life of significance.

While it is true that all human beings are born into sin, are broken vessels, and in desperate need of a Savior to cleanse us from sin, salvation is so much more than clearing our way to heaven in the future by and by. Salvation is a daily, here-and-now experience, which does not just begin on that glorious "great gettin' up day." It appears we can trust God for eternity, but not for the here-and-now of our everyday needs and desires. God the Father, through Jesus Christ, has provided a way to make us whole. To be cleansed of sin and to overcome death is critical in the plan of salvation. However, once we are given new life, the Holy Spirit intends to remove the grave clothes that have bound us and replace them with garments of freedom and praise. Our earthbound Christian journey includes being made whole day-by-day and experiencing new life in Christ.

I invite you to come with me as we journey through the Scriptures and some psychological truths, to discover who we are in Christ and how we can change our outlook and behavior. We will see that no one should have the power to define us except God, our Creator. Our significance is in Him. I trust that as you journey through this book, you will experience the presence and freedom of God's Holy Spirit. I trust that as you read through this work, you will feel the presence of God in a healing way to bring you to salvation, restoration, and significance! There is much to learn, much to change, and much life to live in our salvation.

Chapter 1

The Identity Theft Problem

God created man in His own image, in the image of God He created him; male and female He created them. God blessed them; and God said to them, "Be fruitful and multiply, and fill the earth, and subdue it."
—Genesis 1:27-28

Over the last several years, many of us have had to deal with a problem that can be directly related to the high technology aspects of our time. In the past, theft was relegated to property, wallets, purses, bicycles, automobiles, and other items in our homes. Now someone's actually identity can be stolen by simply gaining the individual's social security number, credit card number, or driver's license information. Once our identity is stolen or altered, a number of abuses can take place. We may see purchases on our credit card that we did not authorize. We may have collection agencies call us regarding outstanding bills we did not incur—which happened to me a couple of years ago.

I was contacted to pay an outstanding bill from a company I had never done business with and that was incurred by someone posing as me in Alaska! I have never been to Alaska. I was living in North Carolina at the time. I had to do many things to prove I was who I said I was, such as contact the local authorities and make a police report; contact all the credit reporting agencies; contact my credit card company; and contact the billing company to assure everyone I was not the irresponsible customer who I was being made out to be. All for a bill that was less than sixty dollars!

To this day I don't know how it all happened. It was a frustrating and time-consuming ordeal. The results of such identity theft can be a reduced credit rating, a diminished personal reputation, and a feeling of being violated. Fortunately, after a couple of months I had a positive outcome as the collection agency relented when it realized that I was a victim of identity theft. When someone steals your identity, it may take a while to restore your reputation and to restore who you really are.

The truth is, our identity was first stolen many thousands of years ago. Satan was successful in convincing Adam and Eve that God was not who He said He was and that we were not who God said we were. Adam's first mistake was not checking with his "Authority" to determine the truth.

Since that time in the garden of Eden, all of us have experienced in various ways the feeling that our identity and significance are dependent upon what we do, our performance, or what others do to us, do for us, say about us, or think about us. Abuse, emotional pain, too many external voices speaking to us, confusion, loss, traumatic circumstances, weariness in disappointments, and feelings of neglect can alter how we feel about our world, our God, and ourselves. Somehow, our true identity has been stolen and altered. It is time to "contact the Authority" to get back the truth of who we are.

God created you to be you. He designed you, He made you, He imparted upon you certain gifts and talents, and He desires to empower you. Human beings were designed for three essential things: make an impact; be in relationships; and glorify God. There are many people who have succeeded in accomplishing the first aspect. Unfortunately, many people have made a self-glorifying and destructive impact rather than a community-oriented and positive one. There are many others who believe they can never make an impact no matter what they may have been given to work with. Very few people have been able to make an impact *and* glorify God. Why? I believe it is because we have allowed many experiences and worldly things, not to mention the devil, to steal from us our true significance. Our significance has been impaired by what others have said to or about us or by what they did to us. Sometimes we listen to our own mental "tape recordings" that have derailed our true significance.

Life has a way of taking the wind out of our sails. Essentially, many people have lost heart in the pursuit of who they are and of glorifying God. Ortberg states,

> Psychologists have begun to speak of what is perhaps the largest mental health problem in our day. It is not depression or anxiety, at least not at clinical levels. It is languishing—a failure to thrive. Languishing is the condition of someone who may be able to function but has lost a sense of hope and meaning. Languishing is not the presence of mental illness; it is the absence of mental and emotional vitality . . . weariness of soul. (Ortberg 2010, 30)

Bad relationships, disappointments, emotional pain, and spiritual doubts have wreaked havoc upon our desires to be who God wants us to be. When we lose heart, we lose purpose. When we lose purpose, we lose significance. Life is the inner power to make something happen (Ortberg 2010, 31). If the devil can reduce us to nothing more than just existing, he has won. As long as we languish in the doldrums of what life has done to us, our significance is dead in the water. However, the good news is that Jesus came to save that which was lost (Matt. 18:11). Jesus did not just save us from something—He saved us for something. That is purpose. Jesus also saved us because He values and cherishes us. That is significance!

Every single one of us needs to be encouraged to see ourselves as God sees us. It is about time that we allow God to breathe life into us again, so we can be a "living soul" (Gen. 2:7). It is about time we turn the tables upon the devil's attempts to steal, kill, and destroy our identity. Satan has operated in identity theft long enough.

Human beings are "fearfully and wonderfully made" (Psa. 139:14). In the Judeo-Christian tradition, it is generally believed that we are comprised of spirit, soul, and body. All three components of humanness are intricately intertwined, each effecting the other. May defines the spirit as the "dynamic force of being, that which is given by God and brings the soul into living reality" (May 1992, 7). If we ignore the spiritual aspect of who we are, we ignore the life-giving essence of our identity. McGee states,

> Whether labeled self-esteem or self-worth, the feeling of significance is crucial to man's emotional, spiritual, and social stability and is the driving element within the human spirit. Understanding this single need opens the door to understanding our actions and attitudes (McGee 2003, 11).

The individual personhood, or the self, is defined by the constant relationship between body, soul, and spirit and is impacted by one's environment and genetics, or nurture and nature. The nature versus nurture debate has been ongoing for many centuries, even from the days of Aristotle and Plato. Over time, the debate went back and forth as to which one was the prominent force when it came to human behavior.

Today most scientists and theorists would say both nature and nurture have an effect on the person, although not necessarily an equal effect. Sometimes our physical appearance has more power to define us. Sometimes the way we feel or think about our environment and our experiences will determine how we are defined. Spiritual beliefs and disciplines can also define who we are. Together, these three components—body, soul, and spirit—impact the search for self and significance in our world.

The human self desires peace, happiness, and contentment. We all want to feel good about ourselves. We all want to experience healthy self-worth. All of these are byproducts of our core longings. However, when most people say they are seeking happiness, for example, they are looking for it in what the world can offer. Oftentimes it becomes a pursuit of self-gratifying experiences and worldly trinkets, neither of which provides the true or long-lasting sense of peace, happiness, and contentment we long for. McGee says,

> We must understand that this hunger for self-worth is God-given and can only be satisfied by Him. Our value is not dependent on our ability to earn the fickle acceptance of people but rather its true source is the love and acceptance of God. He created us. He alone knows how to fulfill all our needs (McGee 2003, 11).

Our Source of life, God our Creator, knows each one of us intimately. As a result, He knows what we desire, what we are looking for, and what we need. We are "fearfully and wonderfully made" by Him and He desires to bless His children. Fenelon says,

> It is true that He desires our happiness, but that is neither the chief end of His work nor an end to be compared with that of His glory. It is for His glory only that He wills our happiness. Happiness is a subordinate consideration that he assigns to the final and essential end of His glory (Fenelon 1997, 33).

When God our Father blesses us, such blessings ultimately bring Him glory. When we walk in our true significance, namely reflecting His image, we bring glory to the Father. Jesus taught, "You are the light of the world . . . Let your light shine before men in such as way that they may see your good works, and glorify your Father who is in heaven" (Matt. 5:14-16).

The way to obtain identity and significance begins with our surrender to God. His love for us, His desire to bless us, His delight in us will lead us into discovering our true selves. God not only brings us significance, He *is* our significance. Anything else we may be attached to or that we desire to bring us our identity means little in comparison.

In addition to being a minister and counselor, I have had the privilege of being an adjunct professor at a Christian college. One of the classes I teach is about the aspects of interpersonal relationships. In order to have good interpersonal relationships, an individual needs to begin with the self. While this may seem a bit odd, the truth is we cannot have healthy relationships if we do not have a healthy view of ourselves.

If we feel good about ourselves and if we know who we are, then the chances of better relationships increase. "How we feel about ourselves is the driving force behind many of our thoughts and actions" (Kirwan 1984, 105). I am not suggesting we think of ourselves as the greatest thing since sliced bread. There is a balance to self-awareness, which I discuss in Chapter 7. When we have a good self-worth, we can view others with acceptance, encouragement, and value, and we take ownership of our own shortcomings. Basically, we can only give what we have!

Most would agree that there are several forces that define the self. May states, "It is good to recognize that we are many-faceted gems" (May 1992, 138). We can be defined by the *culture* in which we live and to which we belong. A person can be defined as Asian, European, Scandinavian, Latino, or American, to name a few. Each one of these cultures has characteristics that influence the thinking and behavior of an individual, which in turn helps define a person.

Other forces that can define the self are certain *physical aspects*. The height, weight, skin color, hair texture, and even handicap of an individual can be an identifying aspect. When a witness to a crime is questioned about what he or she observed, often the witness begins with a physical description to help identify the suspect. Being tall, short, athletic, blond, male, or female are just a few characteristics that are used to define at least part of a person's identity.

Psychological aspects can also describe a person. Psychological aspects would include one's temperament, intelligence, personality, mood, and approach to life as defining factors. A person can be described as shy, smart, or confident. In mental health, as in medical health, a diagnosis is needed in order to submit billing and to develop a treatment plan for someone. A diagnosis is one way to identify an aspect of an individual. The Diagnostic and Statistical Manual of Mental Disorders, Fifth Edition, or the DSM-V, is the resource that is used to obtain a mental health diagnosis. Sometimes a diagnosis is accurate and sometimes it is not. For example, someone can be defined as "bipolar," or "ADHD," or having a "borderline personality disorder." These labels often identify an individual, but we need to be careful as to the impact of such a label. Dr. Gerald May, a psychiatrist and spiritual director, adds his wisdom:

> It would be helpful, I think, to recognize that these labels are in many ways quite accurate, but they are also just labels. They reveal something about the attributes, but nothing of the essence of a person. They describe certain characteristics and conditions, but they do not really address the soul (May 1992, 150).

Our identity is empowered by a loving God, despite how sick and broken we may be. We all need redemption and the healing of our brokenness in order to return to God and to the person He created us to be.

An individual can also be labeled an "alcoholic" or a "drug addict." These labels can be problematic, but our society seems to accept them to categorize people nevertheless. One of the slogans of Alcoholics Anonymous (AA) is, "Once an alcoholic, always an alcoholic." While I understand the intent of this slogan, and the fact that an ex-addict needs to be vigilant in his or her recovery, I personally do not believe it is entirely true. Once Jesus delivers someone from any bondage, that individual becomes new and is given a new name with which to be identified. "Therefore if anyone is in Christ, he is a new creature; the old things passed away; behold new things have come" (2 Cor. 7:17).

Finally, there is another force that shapes the self that is often overlooked and sometimes rejected. It is the *spiritual force*. We are all spirit-beings, according to Scripture, and this is an essential part of who we are. Below are a few examples:

- Proverbs 20:27—"The spirit of man is the lamp of the Lord, searching all the innermost parts of his being."

- Job 32:8—"For there is a spirit in man, and the breath of the Almighty gives them understanding."

- Eccl. 12:7—"Then the dust will return to the earth as it was, and the spirit will return to God who gave it."

- Romans 8:16—"The Spirit Himself testifies with our spirit that we are children of God."

- I Cor. 2:11—"For who among men knows the thoughts of a man except the spirit of the man which is in him?"

Science has long believed that man and some beasts, namely chimpanzees, have come from the same ancestors about 5-7 millions of years ago (McHenry 2009, 265). This origin is thought to be random from an assembly of bacteria, amino acids, and chemicals. The ultimate result of such theories is, in reality, the dehumanization of man. If human beings were randomly formed, then mankind insignificantly came into existence, with very little else than animalistic impulses. We are told in many cultures, including our own, that human beings have evolved from *lower* forms of life, or that we can be "reincarnated" into subsequent higher forms of existence eventually. Not much hope or significance, if you ask me. As a result, the sanctity of human life is ultimately devalued.

Today in our world, people are often more concerned about protecting certain species of animals than they are about protecting our children and the unborn children. Why? I believe that human life is not valued as it would be if we only knew in whose image we are created and the spiritual essence of our being. The ease that seems to exist to abuse and destroy human life, and our children in particular, is the result of a belief system that devalues human life. "What happens in a culture where the dividing line between man and animal are blurry? The answer is: The two blend into one. People lose their sense of humanity, and act more like animals than men" (Overman 199, 60-61). This is the ultimate work of Satan, who seeks to "steal and kill, and destroy" (John 10:10). The only antidote is to believe in the Supreme Creator who gives us life and deems us significant enough to reflect His image.

Genesis indicates that all the beasts of creation were formed "out of the ground" (Gen. 1:24, 2:19). Man too was formed from "the dust of the ground" (Gen. 2:7), so in a unique sense, humans do indeed have a common ancestor with the animal world. It is called dirt! However, there is a major difference. As we continue reading Genesis 2:7 we discover something unique about man—that God, "breathed into his nostrils the breath of life; and man became a living being." The Hebrew words, "ruwach" and "nshamah", are translated as *breath* and *spirit* throughout the Old Testament and are often used interchangeably. The Greek word, "pneuma", also means both *breath* and *spirit*. Part of being in God's image and being identified with Him is to recognize that the giver of life has breathed His life into us. If we can get hold of this truth, it can change how we define who we are and the value we place on human life. "Without spirit, neither body nor soul has life" (Anderson 2000, 24). We do not originate from an ape, or a monkey, or an amoeba—our essential identity comes from Almighty God Himself!

Why is this important? Because, Acts 17:28 declares, "For in Him we live and move and have our being" (RSV). Benner states,

> A complete knowing of our self in relation to God includes knowing three things: our self as deeply loved, our self as

deeply sinful, and our self as in a process of being redeemed and restored. Facing these deep truths about ourselves makes it possible for us to accept and know ourselves as we are accepted and known by God (Benner 2004, 72).

All three of these truths, that we are deeply loved, that we are deeply sinful and we are in the process of redemption impacts our ability to find fulfillment. However, the answers do not lie in what the world can bring, nor do they lie within fallen humanity. Calvin wrote, "There is no deep knowing of God without a deep knowing of self and no deep knowing of self without a deep knowing of God" (Calvin 1995, 15). To truly know who we are, we need to know God, for we reflect Him. "Man is free when his life is shaped according 'to the image of God,' that is, when he knows that he is living on the power of God, on the gift of God" (Brunner 1947, 170). As we look to find God, we will find ourselves.

All of us have an innate sense that there is something or someone beyond ourselves who can provide meaning. This is especially true when we face doubt and pain. Crabb states:

> Pain makes people stand still and think about something outside of themselves, something more important and more interesting than their own concerns about who they are and how they are getting on. Pain compels people to ask terrifying questions about themselves, life, and God (Crabb 2006, 34).

I have heard many individuals claim they are a "spiritual" person. Such people are acknowledging there is something within them that cannot be explained or satisfied by conventional means. Many of these people read philosophical books, may or may not attend church, meditate on who knows what, and perhaps may or may not believe in God, all in pursuit of the deep meaning of their life and being "spiritual." "There is no such thing as our 'spiritual life' and then our 'real life.' It is all one" (Cloud and Townsend 2001, 21).

Human core longings have been created to be part of our spirit as our spirit is seeking to connect to something or someone to bring identity to our life. That should tell us something. It tells me our longings for identity come from our spirit-man and therefore can only be met by the One who breathed our spirit into being. Scripture teaches this truth. As noted earlier, Job 32:8 says, "For there is a spirit in man, and the breath of the Almighty gives them understanding." In Ecclesiastes 12:7 we read, "Then the dust will return to the earth as it was, and the spirit will return to God who gave it."

Discovering our identity can be a lifelong adventure. However, it usually begins when we are young. During adolescence, identity and the feelings of significance are emerging as important aspects in the life of the young person. "Research indicates that identity status profoundly influences an adolescent's social expectations, self-image, and reaction to stress (Craig 1996, 439). These life circumstances and "statuses," as James Marcia calls them, contribute to a person's identity. James E. Marcia has done extensive research on identity development during adolescence and throughout the human life span. Dr. Marcia is a clinical and developmental psychologist, has held professorships in U.S. and Canadian universities, and is currently an Emeritus Professor of Psychology at Simon Fraser University in British Columbia, Canada. Dr. Marcia developed what he called the *Four Statuses of Identity*. His theory of identity achievement states there are two distinct parts contributing to the achievement of adolescent identity: a *time of choosing or crisis*, and a *commitment*. Dr. Marcia's four statuses are:

- **Identity Diffusion**—not yet had crisis/time of choosing or commitment; maybe undecided or uninterested; since no understanding of one's identity exists and no choice is being made at this time, there is no corresponding commitment.
- **Identity Foreclosure**—made a commitment but with no exploration; forced commitments from parents and others. One's identity is expected to be what someone else says it is. There is a commitment, albeit a reluctant one, but choice is made for us.
- **Identity Moratorium**—in the midst of a crisis or exploration, but vague or no commitment. A person may be in a crisis trying to find a solution or may be exploring several interests and ideas, but there is no commitment yet toward the direction of a decision.
- **Identity Achievement**—Eureka! Finished exploring and have made commitment. Identity has been discovered, based upon a person's discovery of his or her passion, calling, or destiny. Once found, he or she pursues with commitment. (Craig 1996, 439)

While it is common and easy to identify ourselves by what we do, in reality it is just a small part of our identity. We often make what we do our entire identity. The truth is defining who we are encompasses much more than simply what we do. Our significance is measured by so much more. We are human *beings*, not human *doings*.

Ultimately, our deep desires often help identify who we are. These deep desires, or *core longings*, exist in every human being. Core longings, which will be discussed in the next chapter, are desires that have been created to be *primarily* satisfied in relationship, first and foremost in relationship to God. Then *secondarily*, the Lord provides human relationships in which these longings can be partially satisfied with one another. "People need two sorts of relationships to grow: the divine and the human" (Cloud and Townsend 2001, 81).

The problem has been that when sin came into the human experience, separation from God occurred. When Adam and Eve sinned, a colossal problem developed. Broken relationship between God and humans brought the inability for man to satisfy the core longings that were created in him. Laaser states, "Underneath every problem there is always an unfulfilled desire" (Laaser 2008, 41). Halley says, "Behind, under, and in every wound is a core-longing deficit" (Halley, 2008). When separation from God occurred, *the core longings did not go away.* The devil simply convinced us they can be satisfied by our own doing and selfish pursuits, without God. This is the essence of our "identity theft," if you will. When we commit sin, or when sin and evil happen to us, human beings will look for relief toward, and fulfillment of, these longings any way we can.

Men and women are good at trying to *avoid* pain at all costs. In reality, the problem is that completely avoiding pain is impossible on this fallen earth. So if pain cannot be completely avoided, we will often look for ways to *ignore* pain; *repress* pain; or *medicate* pain. Emotionally wounded people will often grasp onto bad relationships, addictions, or whatever the world offers to find pleasure, to satisfy their desires, to find fulfillment, and to define themselves in ways that are unsustainable.

We all continued to long for the fulfillment of the important internal needs with which we were created. However, we all were left with separation from the true *primary* way to meet their inner needs—through relationship with God. "Self-fulfillment is an intrinsic need and positive good for every person. It is when self-fulfillment becomes a craving for indulging the self that the craziness and chaos begins" (Anderson 2000, 39). The result is that men and women begin to search and attempt to meet the core longings through other means and through their own efforts. May concurs when he states:

> We seek our deepest meaning in what we can achieve through the work of our own hands. Even more often we kill our inner longing by dulling our awareness with tranquilizers, alcohol, food, work, and the host of behavioral sedations that we falsely call recreation. True recreation, like true rest, leaves us with greater energy and clearer awareness. But when we narcotize ourselves, regardless of the means, we are left clouded and sapped of strength. (May 1992, 6)

This self-driven pursuit develops into countless harmful behaviors, self-centeredness, perversion, pain, substance abuse, addictions, and disappointment, to name a few. Wardle suggests ways in which the world answers core longings:

- Idolatry is substituted for fellowship with God.
- Money and power are thought to bring security and safety.
- Personal performance is linked to self-worth.
- Approval replaces uniqueness.
- Position now determines importance.
- Sexual activity is substituted for genuine love.
- Godless pleasure is thought to bring lasting enjoyment.
- Career advancement is pushed as the answer to fulfillment in life. (Wardle 2005, 65-6)

The ultimate result is we are trying to find our identity through anything or anyone except God. God's plan of redemption through Jesus Christ provides the only way in which we can once again experience fulfillment of the deep desires we long for.

So, who or what defines a person? For example, it can be addictions, codependent relationships, material things, emotional wounds, physical conditions, the praises of man, and worldly pursuits. These things that often define us are twisted attempts to meet the deep longings in the human soul. Whether we admit it or not, our core longings can never be *completely* met by human beings or worldly pursuits. People and the world will often let us down and fall short of being able to meet all of our needs. If we were honest, we could all admit we have been disappointed in our pursuits.

Worldly pursuits lack the ability to completely satisfy a person's core longings. Are we looking for other things and people to make us feel significant? If so, we need to know that nothing will be able to maintain the lasting significance that we seek. External things will not satisfy the internal longings of our souls as Jesus can. I agree with Anderson when he points out, "that this dualism within the self between the physical and nonphysical is the root of anxiety as the core of most mental and emotional illness" (Anderson 2000, 36). Addictive pursuits are fleeting, harmful, and even deadly. Since God created the longings of the human soul, only He can completely meet and fulfill them.

The next chapter will introduce the six core longings.

Chapter 2
Core Longings

*My soul thirsts for You; my flesh longs for You in a dry
and thirsty land where there is no water.*
Psalm 63:1 (NKJV)

*Hope deferred makes the heart sick,
but a longing fulfilled is a tree of life.*
Proverbs 13:12 (NIV).

One of my favorite television shows of all time was *Happy Days* (1974-84), especially with the original cast. Henry Winkler portrayed Arthur Fonzarelli, and he was also known as "Fonzi" or "the Fonz." He was the neighborhood street rat, biker dude, and tough guy and everyone was afraid of him. He was rough around the edges and often seemed to be ready for a fight to defend his turf and reputation. His identity was wrapped up in his "presentation," if you will, and his reputation. As the characters developed over the years, something interesting happened. Fonzi developed a friendship with an unlikely character—Richie Cunningham. Richie was the son of a middle-class, all-American family depicted in the show.

He was a good student, an average athlete, and a popular kid. The unlikely relationship between Fonzi and Richie grew to include other members of the Cunningham family.

Eventually, Richie's mother, Marion Cunningham, had a unique effect upon Fonzi. She was depicted as a loving, devoted, and simple down-to-earth mother and wife. She was not intimidated by "the Fonz" at all. His reputation did not seem to sway her. She dealt with him like she treated everyone else. She even got away with calling him "Arthur." Had anyone else called him by his real name, he or she would have felt Fonzi's wrath. Fonzi began to let his guard down and to feel comfortable in the Cunningham's home. He felt he was *understood*; he felt *loved*; he felt *safe* enough to allow his rough persona to melt in the presence of the Cunninghams; he had a renewed *purpose* to be a blessing to his community instead of being a problem to the neighborhood; he had a family to whom he felt a sense of *belonging*; and he felt *significant* to a group of people he grew to care about and who encouraged his gifts to emerge from his life. The Fonz was transformed through the realization of his human core longings and by how they were met in an environment that accepted him and empowered him to be Arthur, not just Fonzi.

I loved this show because of Fonzi's transformation, and how such transformation created and enhanced relationships. At times, the show brought me to tears as I witnessed the character change in such a dramatic way and watched the development of meaningful relationships between the Cunninghams and "the Fonz." To be sure, Fonzi still kept much of his tough-guy persona, but he became a go-to guy, not someone to avoid.

I accepted Jesus Christ as my personal Savior while a freshman in college, just about the time *Happy Days* went on the air. I did not know it then, but as I continued to enjoy the show *Happy Days*, I was emotionally responding to the need in my own life for those same core longings to be met. As God was ministering to me and changing me, I developed a growing desire to see others be transformed by His Spirit as well. Years later I moved into many aspects of ministry, such as music ministry, leading worship, preaching, counseling, administration, the prophetic gifts, and teaching. A passion developed to encourage transformation in the lives of people I ministered to. It developed into a focus upon the counseling, educating, and empowering ministry into which God has ultimately led me. I found that addressing just the symptoms and behaviors were not enough. The root of human brokenness can only be reached, healed, and restored by God. My role is to position people who are experiencing soul hurts to encounter healing and transformation through God's Holy Spirit.

I believe there are essentially six core longings: *love, safety, understanding, belonging, purpose, and significance.* Regardless of culture, ethnicity, age, or gender, these core longings exist in every human spirit. One or more of these core longings may be especially strong depending on a person's background, temperament, and personality. There also can be some overlap between these core longings, as they are intertwined within every human being.

Created in the image of God, we were made to reflect God relationally (spiritually, socially, and through self-awareness), rationally (images and beliefs), volitionally (motivations and actions), emotionally (responses and reactions), and in our physical activities. God's desire is for the whole person, and He desires to fulfill these human core longings. From the beginning God established these longings in the lives of Adam and Eve, and they both found fulfillment of these core longings and completeness in God, and then in each other. Core longings are meant to draw us into God's embrace, resulting in rest and contentment. When Adam and Eve transgressed against the

Lord's boundaries for their lives, the relationship between them was greatly affected as well. When the source of human definition, the Lord Himself, became separated from Adam and Eve through their sin, the way they saw each other was also impacted.

When parents, who may have missed out on the proper fulfillment of their own core longings, mistreat their own children, pain and woundedness occurs. If a youngster was physically or sexually abused, the child's desire for love, safety, and understanding is greatly impacted and negatively affected. If a child is constantly ridiculed or neglected, the child's desire for belonging, purpose, and significance are often negatively affected and driven out of proportion. Since these core longings do not go away, a wounded person will seek ways to meet these deep desires. Woundedness and pain, however, greatly cloud our ability to meet such desires in healthy and fulfilling ways. It also impacts the way we identify and define ourselves. Wardle says,

> Deep wounds impact what she believes about herself and her world. The experience of insensitivity and abuse at such an early age can lead to serious distorted thinking. This is particularly true when the adults who are called to care for a person actually injure her. The child is far too young to process all that happens, and there is nowhere to turn for help. Strong emotions lead her to draw conclusions about life based on what she has seen and experienced. (Wardle 2001, 45)

This, of course, is true of boys as well as girls. All youngsters, and adults for that matter, are positively or negatively affected by their environment.

Adam and Eve felt guilt and shame and tried to hide from God and each other (Gen. 3:7-8). They experienced a broken relationship, and they looked to blame God and each other for the brokenness.

"Simply put, shame is a feeling of being inwardly flawed—of not measuring up" (Wright 2005, 19). Essentially, guilt says, "I did something bad." Shame says, "I am bad." When we experience shame, we want to hide. After all, if we are so flawed, who would want to be with us? The truth is we are not flawed—we are broken. Being flawed is when the item is not made well. We all were made in God's image. We were divinely designed. Being broken is when the item needs to be fixed. It would work fine if it was simply restored to what it was supposed to be and do.

Jesus came to "fix" our brokenness so we can be who we were created to be. Sin broke us, but Jesus took care of sin and restored us to our true identity. While it is true that we can't measure up to God in our sin and brokenness, the finished work of Christ makes a way for us to be restored to right relationship with God. God remains in the restoration business today through His Son, our Savior, Jesus Christ.

When Adam and Eve realized they sinned and tried to hide from God, God asked several profound questions of Adam.

> They heard the sound of the Lord God walking in the garden in the cool of the day, and the man and his wife hid themselves from the presence of the Lord God among the trees of the garden. Then the Lord God called to the man, and said to him, *"Where are you?"* He said "I heard the sound of You in the garden, and I was afraid because I was naked; so I hid myself." And He said, *"Who told you that you were naked? Have you eaten from the tree of which I commanded you not to eat?"* (Gen. 3:8-11, emphasis added)

Two of the questions God asked are significant for our discussion. Notice that when God called out to Adam, He did not ask, *"Who are you?"* *Who* Adam was, was not in question. Adam and Eve were still made in God's image. Adam was still God's son, and Eve was still God's daughter. Their standing in creation was secure as God's stewards. However, a great separation took place. Instead, God asked, "*Where* are you?" The Old Testament Hebrew phrase can be rendered, "How did you get here?" The question the Lord asked was more of a reflection of the changed *relationship* in which Adam and Eve found themselves.

The tone of God's questions is also important. The Lord's tone was not a finger-in-your-face critical tone. It was one of a Father wondering how His son allowed separation to occur between them. It was as if God was asking, "How did you get to this point where you doubted my love and care for you?" It was coming from a Father whose heart was broken because He too experienced separation.

When God asked, "Who told you that you were naked?," He was asking in the same loving tone. It was as if God was saying to Adam, "Who told you such a thing? It surely was not me. I thought you knew where you stood with me. Did you eat from the forbidden tree? It breaks my heart that you believed someone else over my loving and caring intentions for you."

The devil was successful in portraying to Adam and Eve a very different God than the One who created them and covered them in His identity and love. I will discuss this further in Chapter 4. When parents experience estrangement from their children, for example, the fact that they are still parents and the children are still their children does not change. Often, children have believed their own, or someone else's assessment of their parents intentions, which results in a negative view of their parents. Once this belief seeps into a young person's mind, it can lead to a broken relationship.

The Lord still desired to love and define His children. The first humans longed for their suddenly lost relationship with God. Adam's sin separated him from God. Adam and Eve felt distance, fear, and shame—even between each other. Their shame was why they hid from God. The feeling of shame replaced the feeling of significance. So the Lord developed a plan of redemption in order to restore relationship with mankind and to satisfy the longings for identity and fulfillment in human beings. This plan of redemption is through the finished, healing, restoring, and saving work of Jesus Christ.

The Garden of Paradise

The garden of Eden was made as a place of peace and provision for mankind. Adam and Eve had it all. The most important aspect that they had was an unbroken, intimate relationship with their Creator, the lover of their souls. They were identified by His name. Adam and Eve enjoyed perfect peace and provision as they served God and one another. After the six days of creation, God said things were very good (Gen. 1:10, 12, 18, 21, 25, and 31). The only caveat was that God acknowledged that it was *not* good for man to be alone (Gen. 2:18). This speaks to the first core longing in human beings—a sense of *belonging*.

Attachment to something or someone brings identity, connectedness, and a sense of value. We can all think of important things or people we are attached to. As a high school and college athlete, I remember the feeling of being a part of a team. Being in the race together. Being in the game together. Knowing you were not alone was huge in team building and in life. People feel a sense of belonging when they are simply cheering for the same team and "wearing the colors." Membership in college fraternities and sororities are popular activities for many—for those who want to belong to something. College alumni associations bank on the fact that graduates will feel a certain attachment to their alma mater when a call is made to solicit contributions.

Do you ever wonder why our culture is so big on college and professional sports? Why do we see so many avid fans go to many lengths just to be with others who share their passion for their team? Also, why is there, especially among young people, a growing membership in street gangs? Approximately 1.4 million active street gang, outlaw motorcycle gang, and prison gang members, comprising more than 33,000 gangs, are criminally active within all 50 US states, the District of Columbia, and Puerto Rico. This represents a 40 percent increase from an estimated one million gang members in 2009 (FBI, 2011). Why? My personal belief is that we have seen such a growing devotion to teams, groups, and fraternal organizations because it provides a sense of belonging among others, perhaps as a result of the breakdown of the family—the ultimate entity that brings a sense of belonging. Laaser says, "The desire to be included starts with the desire in our soul to belong to a family" (Laaser 2008, 38). A future edition of the series, *Created for Belonging*, will discuss this core longing in more detail.

Adam and Eve also experienced *love*, especially unconditional love. To be loved *and* express and give love is another core longing in human beings. Reciprocated love is essential in the love experience. Love brings aspects such as acceptance, embrace, delight, action, and preference. God provided love to Adam and Eve by the way He equipped them, cherished them, delighted in them, and protected and provided for them. "The generative love of God was our origin. The embracing love of God sustains our existence. The inextinguishable love of God is the only hope for our fulfillment" (Benner 2004, 49).

Adam and Eve in turn loved God, which was indicated through their devotion to Him, their appreciation of His provisions for their lives, and their willingness to serve God by cultivating His creation. More will be explored about love and relationships in the forthcoming book, *Created for Love*.

God also enjoyed spending time with them, and His presence was constant, unhindered prior to the fall. Someone's constant affirming presence provides another human core longing: *safety* or security. The Lord's presence brought security, protection, guidance, and provision. Safety provides a sense of peace, a resulting benefit of feeling safe. The Bible uses the concept of "covering" to depict the consequences of being under cover. There are also consequences in choosing to walk out from under a covering. More about the aspect of safety will be discussed in *Created for Covering*.

For our discussion right now, allow me to mention briefly some thoughts about the desire for safety. Human beings deeply long for safety and the sense of well-being. "When the desire for safety is met, we feel a certain freedom and confidence to explore the world and even take a few risks" (Laaser 2008, 28). Laaser adds, "Sometimes problems we had in the past lead us to have undue concern for our safety" (Laaser 2008, 29). When safety and security is not assured, communication is hindered and even shut down. After all, can I feel safe to share my thoughts and feelings without being ridiculed or insulted?

Men and women will do whatever they can to find safety and peace. When peace is not found, people will seek it, often using their own means. However, a person's attempts often bring disappointment, danger, and harm. It is in the presence of God that a person will ultimately find safety.

Safety and security are results of trust. I define trust as believing someone has *your* best interest at heart. Adam and Eve had complete trust in God and in each other, prior to the advent of sin. It was evident there was no attempt to do for themselves what God had already done and was doing for them. All of their needs were being met.

Genesis 1:29 tells us what God did for Adam and Eve: "And God said, 'See, I have given you every herb that yields seed which is on the face of all the earth, and every tree whose fruit yields seed; to you it shall be for food.'" There was apparently no longing for their needs. The one exception was that God told Adam and Eve to avoid the tree of the knowledge of good and evil (Gen. 2:16-17). This was for their protection and for their safety. All mankind needed to know about good and evil came from a *relationship* with God.

God told them they would die if they ate from the tree. Satan said they would not die. Who should have been believed? Satan will adorn death to make it look appealing and desirable. The essence of the devil's temptation to Adam and Eve was for them to take on for themselves what only God could rightfully provide. It was as if Satan was telling Adam and Eve that God was holding out on them by prohibiting them from the one tree.

As long as we believe we have the power, *apart* from God, to gain knowledge, wisdom, significance, and purpose, we will ultimately miss the mark and become quite disappointed. As Proverbs says, "The fear of the Lord is the beginning of knowledge," (Pro. 1:7). Also, Proverbs 9:10 adds, "The fear of the Lord is the beginning of wisdom."

God also provided *purpose* to Adam and Eve. Having purpose brings out important aspects such as direction, empowerment, and dependability. Scriptures do not indicate the length of time Adam and Eve existed before the serpent came to tempt them. However, for a period of time, it was clear God gave Adam and Eve the purpose and responsibility to have dominion over God's creation. He delegated to the first couple the empowerment to, "Be fruitful and multiply, and fill the earth, and subdue it; and rule . . ." God clearly tells them, "I have given you . . ."

The giving to mankind by God has been consistent from the outset. When God gives to man, purpose is also given. When we take for ourselves, we are pursuing a false purpose. Man was empowered and directed to fulfill a great purpose. Our longing for purpose continues today. People want to know why they are here and what their purpose may be. Apart from God's provision and direction, individuals will attempt to determine their purpose using selfish, worldly, and ultimately disappointing means. God has a purpose for each one of us, and only through relationship with Him will we find it. *Created for Purpose* will further discuss finding our purpose.

Human beings also have the longing to be *understood*. Understanding breeds knowledge and intimacy. We have so many things to say. We want to be seen. We are born to communicate (Laaser 2008, 18). We want others to understand us. For another person to understand us, he or she would need to know our thoughts, tendencies, intentions, feelings, desires, and personality.

Many of my friends and I were raised with the old saying, "It is better for children to be seen and not heard." In the minds of some people, the connotation was that children needed to behave and be respectful. However, there are better ways to communicate this truth. More often, this cliché gave the message that children have no voice. Children do have a voice. They should also be respectful and obedient, but they have a voice. On the other hand, children often say their parents "just don't get it" about aspects of their lives.

Sometimes that is true, but more often than not the kids do not understand the motives of the parents and what their parents know about life. A lack of understanding of both perspectives becomes a gap in communication.

Someone also needs to listen. Listening is the most important aspect of communication in all relationships. Listening is not just waiting for our turn to speak—to *listen* means to *understand* what is being communicated. There is a difference between hearing and listening. We can *hear* sounds, noises, and voices. Listening is the understanding of the specific sounds and what is being said.

My wife is an avid bird watcher. She amazingly can identify a bird by is shape, size and colors. She also listens to the bird sounds. When she hears a bird, she listens intently. She understands the sound and can identify the type of bird she hears. When I hear a bird, I just hear a bird sound. Most of the time, I am not able to identify the type of bird I am hearing, because I do not understand the distinct sound.

It is frustrating and even hurtful when we feel misunderstood. One important goal in a marriage is for each spouse to understand or know each other. When understanding occurs, relational aspects such as communication in marriage, the meeting of each other's needs, and sexual fulfillment are enhanced. The Bible makes it clear that God truly understands men and women. Scripture says, "For we do not have a high priest who cannot sympathize with our weaknesses, but One who has been tempted in all things as we are, yet without sin" (Heb. 4:15).

Jesus also experienced grief, betrayal, rejection, scorn, abuse, false accusations, frustration, doubt, anger, misunderstanding, and demanding expectations. Seamands writes,

> "Jesus suffered injustice, felt the shame of nakedness, was deprived of his rights, endured taunting, was the focus of others' rage, and was rejected and forsaken. He also endured excruciating physical pain, thirst, hunger, emptiness, torment, confusion, and finally death itself" (Seamands 2003, 16).

Jesus surely knows our plights in life. He understands our pain, disappointments, and fears. "For consider Him who endured such hostility from sinners against Himself, lest you become weary and discouraged in your souls" (Heb. 12:3). Being wounded causes us to lose heart. Consider Jesus. He understands and wants to restore you. Seek Him while He is to be found, and He will restore your soul. Further examination of being understood will be presented in the book *Created for Understanding*.

Another core longing in human beings is that of *significance*, which will be the focus of this book, the first in a series. The dictionary defines significance as "full of purpose" or "important." Significance means the importance or the meaning of something or someone. In other words, significance is related to our identity. It provides the understanding of uniqueness. Significance emphasizes the *value* of each individual. We all have a desire to feel important to someone or to a purpose.

Significance is essentially the result of purpose being played out. The world says, our identity is based upon what we do. Our fallen world has it backwards. True significance is when we are valued for who we are.

Significance provides a healthy sense of self and the motivation to make an impact, to enjoy one's accomplishments, to experience self-fulfillment, and to impart to others attributes and things that are important. Significance rests in who we are, not just what we do!

Significance is played out in relationships, our spheres of influence, and the world around us. Significance is seen when we are able to influence someone because of our example or when we make an impact. Significance is felt when we know we are valued and when we receive affirmations, compliments, and encouragement.

However, because our world is becoming increasingly critical and cynical, many people seek significance through sinful and dangerous means. "Self-fulfillment is an intrinsic need and positive good for every person. It is when self-fulfillment becomes a craving for indulging the self that the craziness and chaos begins" (Anderson 2000, 39). Some individuals have more of an impact than others, but this usually does not matter if we are feeling fulfilled and affirmed in our calling. When we are fulfilled and have a level of significance, we will feel a sense of peace.

More importantly, we feel significant to someone when we are in a healthy, loving relationship. True, foundational and long-lasting significance comes from knowing that someone chooses to love us for who we are, not just because of what we do. Significance should not be completely based upon performance and accomplishments—it is essentially based upon our standing in relationship. We know we are significant when we feel love, acceptance and affirmation from someone else. If we feel secure in our relationship with a special someone, we know we are significant. When the standing is in question, we will tend to obtain our significance through our own accomplishments, imbalanced relationships, and dangerous pursuits, to name a few. Therefore, it is essential to be in relationship with God, and enjoy the sense of knowing how He feels about us.

Adam and Eve had tremendous significance to God. He blessed them. He cherished them. God made it clear to Adam and Eve that because of their relationship with Him, they were to have dominion over all creation and for them to be fruitful and to multiply (Gen. 1:28). Their significance in God was supposed to lead to righteous success.

I pray that as you explore this book, and this series, you will find newness in your life. Your true identity is at stake. Your approach to life is at stake. Let us continue to learn the importance of relationship with God through Jesus Christ as the primary means of fulfillment and empowerment!

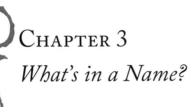

Chapter 3
What's in a Name?

And there is salvation in no one else; for there is no other name under heaven that has been given among men by which we must be saved.
Acts 4:12

The song "Jesus, Name Above All Names" is a simple worship chorus that indicates the unique power and importance of our Savior's name. Very few families of the world name their child "Jesus." In the Hispanic tradition, Jesus is found as a relatively common name to give to a son. However, other cultures seem to refrain from giving their sons the name. There is a unique identity assigned to that name.

The prophetic aspect in the biblical culture underscores the importance of identity that is often provided through names. Old and New Testaments are replete with the importance of one's identity given through their names or where they are from. Often, a better identity or destiny was called forth by giving or changing a person's name. Jesus changed Simon's name to Peter, (Matt. 16:18). Simon means "a stone" while Peter means "rock." Jesus was indicating that the impetuous and compulsive Simon would eventually be a strong and steady individual in the challenging ministry of the Gospel. In the end, Peter was later martyred for his preaching and his steadfast faith.

Allow me to use a story from ancient Greek mythology to illustrate how an incorrect identity can change everything. The war between Troy and Sparta was allegedly begun over the abduction of Helen, who was the wife of Menelaus, the king of Sparta. Paris, the prince of Troy, fell in love with Helen and abducted her and brought her to Troy. After kidnapping Helen, Paris refused to return her, and Menelaus gathered an army and invaded Troy. The story of the Trojan horse arose from this invasion.

Throughout the history of Greek mythology, Helen was known as Helen of Troy. Yet she was actually from Sparta and had been married to the king of Sparta. She is not known as Helen of Sparta—she is known as Helen of Troy. She became known by the city that was not her home. She became known through her *bondage*—not her significance as a queen. She was identified by her *captivity*, not by her true place of citizenship!

I declare to you that you are not to be known by your captivity and bondage. Rather, through the love and finished work of Jesus, you can be known by His name. You can be known by a new identity in Christ. You can be significant in Him!

In the Old Testament, there are many recorded examples of names being prophetically given or changed. For example, the name Abram means "father" or "high father." God later changed his name to "Abraham," which means "father of a multitude." His name was changed as a prophetic indication of God's calling upon Abram to be the father of many nations (Gen. 17:5).

As an angel, the devil was named Lucifer before he was cast out of heaven. Lucifer is one of only three angels who are identified by name in the Scriptures, the other two being Gabriel and Michael. Gabriel means "God is my strength" and Michael means "Who is like God." Lucifer's name means "star of the morning" or simply "bright one" (Isa. 14:12). Upon his expulsion from the heavenly realms (Isa. 14:12-15; Eze. 28:13-17; Rev. 12:7-9), Lucifer's name was changed to Satan (Job 1:6, 2:1), which means "adversary." Satan's role and standing before God changed dramatically, and as a result, so did his name and identity. Ever since that time, Satan has indeed become the adversary of God and the enemy of the people of God.

Some other examples of prophetic meanings of names would be Adam, Seth, Isaac, Jacob, and Methuselah. The name Adam means "from the red earth." Adam was formed from "the dust of the ground' (Gen. 2:7).

Seth was the third son of Adam and Eve. Seth was conceived after Cain killed his brother, Abel. Genesis 4:25 records his birth and that Eve "named him Seth, for she said, 'God has appointed me another offspring in place of Abel, for Cain killed him.'" The name Seth means "substitute."

Isaac was the promised son of Abraham and Sarah. When told by God that they would have a son, Abraham and Sarah laughed. They did not believe it to be possible. The Scriptures record that they were advanced in age, and "Sarah was past childbearing." Yet Sarah conceived and gave birth to a son, just as God promised. The name Isaac means "laughter" (Gen. 18:11-15, 21:5-7).

Then Isaac had two sons, twins named Jacob and Esau. Jacob was born second, holding on to his brother's heel (Gen. 25:26). The name Jacob means "supplanter," which describes one who takes the place of someone else through force or through scheming. As it turned out, Genesis 27 describes how Jacob, with the help of his mother, developed a scheme and successfully tricked Esau out of his given birthright.

However, as God has done with many other individuals in the Bible, He changed Jacob's name to indicate a new definition and destiny. But the change did not come easily. Jacob had to wrestle with God. Through one entire night, Jacob wrestled with God apparently over his guilt of trickery and the ill-gotten blessing from Esau through his own efforts, and an overwhelming fear of Esau. In the morning, God asked Jacob, "What is your name?" (Gen. 32:27). Once Jacob called out his own name, humbly confessing and surrendering to God, the Lord moved in a powerful and positive way. Jacob needed to give up his self-sufficiency. God changed Jacob's name to "Israel," which means "prince with God" (Gen. 32:27-32). Jacob had to "die" before Israel came to "life." Israel reconciled with his brother, Esau (Gen. 33:4), and became the father of twelve sons, who would later become the patriarchs of the twelve tribes of the nation of Israel. A new powerful destiny, indeed!

My favorite biblical name is Methuselah. Methuselah was the father of Lamech and the grandfather of Noah. According to Scripture, he lived to be 969 years old (Gen. 5:25-27), the oldest man who ever lived. His name is prophetic as well, and it means "his death shall bring it" or "when he dies, it will come." The great flood of the Old Testament came soon after Methuselah died!

The Lord also told the Old Testament prophet Hosea to give his children prophetic names. He was to name his daughter Lo-Ruhamah ("no compassion"). Then his youngest son was given the name Lo-Ammi ("not my people"). In a unique way God was speaking through Hosea to convey His anger toward the people of

Israel, who had turned away from God, who were in sin, and who became unfaithful to the Lord.

Job means "persecuted." Not only did Job have a bad stretch of days at the beginning of his story (Job 1 and 2), his friends did more to persecute him than they did to help. Of course God had the final say as to Job's ultimate outcome and destiny, despite his given name, and restored to him two-fold of what he had before his trial began (Job 42:10-13).

Consider the story of John the Baptist. The first chapter of Luke provides the story of the conception and birth of John the Baptist. John's parents were Zacharias and Elizabeth. When Elizabeth gave birth to a son, her relatives and neighbors expected her to name their son Zacharias, after his father. However, Elizabeth made it clear to them that his name was to be John (Luke 13:57-60). The relatives then made an interesting statement, found in verse 61: "And they said to her, 'There is no one among your relatives who is called by that name.'" The expectation was that a family name of some kind was to be given to the child, but it did not happen in John's case. The family name helped identify to whom the child belonged. In this case, however, the name John identified the child as belonging to God. Luke 1:66 states, "For the hand of the Lord was certainly with him. The name John means, "graced by God" or "God is gracious." While a name can provide or hinder a sense of significance, the presence of the Lord in someone's life is the true way in which a person's significance is felt.

Names today, especially exotic names, have become trendy. Many of these names are given because of their meanings. Exotic names are also given as a way to gain attention to both the parents and the child. Then as the child grows, the spotlight shifts to the youngster.

Parents need to be mindful of what their children's names may do for or to their children later in life. A news report a couple of years ago indicated that a couple in New Jersey had named their son "Adolph Hitler," as his first and middle name. That poor child is most likely going to have difficulty throughout his school years and as he becomes an adult. Frank Zappa, a rock musician from the 1960s and '70s named his children Moon Unit and Dweezel. I recently learned that Hollywood actor Jason Lee named his child "Pilot Inspektor." Really, people? Are we not considering our children? If parents name their child using a different or difficult spelling, it may burden the child with having to always spell out the name for the rest of his or her life. The overly creative name may become more of a self-centered statement than what the child had bargained for. Since names have such a powerful influence upon one's identity, parents need to take care with a child's lifelong moniker.

Other cultures throughout the world also understand the importance of names. Names that are given within an ethnic culture may be different to the prevailing culture but often have meanings within their native language. For example, African, Asian, Hispanic, and Slovak names often have meanings that are given to children to encourage a particular future destiny. Parents often want to place a meaningful description of their child upon their life. Other names are given because they are simply different from the rest, as if to say their child will stand out because of their name.

I managed a Christian bookstore for several years, and we often sold books that listed various baby names from A to Z, with their meanings. Over the years Christian parents have become more mindful about how they name their children. Some of today's common names are Joshua, Matthew, Jacob, Rachel, Rebecca, and Jonathan. This was true in our nation during the 1700s and 1800s, as many prominent men and women, including many of our forefathers, had biblical names. There was *Benjamin* Franklin; *John* Adams; *Thomas* Jefferson; *Andrew* Jackson, and of course *Abraham* Lincoln.

God reveals Himself many ways in Scripture. He reveals Himself through creation (Psa. 19:16; Rom. 1:20-12); through the prophets (Heb. 1:1); through the written Word (2 Tim. 3:16; 2 Pet. 1:19-21); through His Son, Jesus Christ (Heb. 1:2); and through His names. God is known as the "Ancient of Days" (Dan. 7:9); the "Good Shepherd" (Psa. 23; John 10:1-21); and the "Alpha and Omega" (Rev.1:8; 21:6; and 22:13).

There is one God, but the many significant names provide us with understanding as to who He is and His nature. Some names are descriptions of God's character while others are more descriptive of His titles. The following are some names of God found in the Bible that will help us develop a glimpse of who God is:

- **El Elyon**—"the most high God" (Psa. 57:2)
- **Elohim**—"God the powerful" (2 Chron. 20:6; Psa. 33:6-11). This name is also found in the early chapters of Genesis. This Hebrew word is plural in its form, thereby indicating the triune nature of God as Father, Son, and Holy Spirit.
- **I Am**—speaks of His self-existing nature and His constant unwavering presence (Exo. 3:14; John 8:58). God has no beginning and no end.
- **El Roi**—"God who sees (me)" (Psa. 34:15; Gen. 16:13-14; Psa. 139).
- **El Shaddai**—"Almighty God" (Psa. 91:1). This name depicts God's unlimited power and resources.
- **Adonai**—"Master" or "our Lord and our God" (Psa. 86:12)
- **Jehovah**—"The Lord (my God)" (Isa. 26:4; Exo. 34:5-7). This name actually depicts the personal nature of God, unlike the idols and other gods of the Old Testament and in history. It is used more than fifty-five hundred times. Jehovah appears when relationship between God and people are involved.

- **Jehovah-Rohi**—"The Lord our Shepherd" (Psa. 23; Isa. 40:11; John 10:11)
- **Jehovah-Shalom**—"The Lord our Peace" (Isa. 9:6; Judg. 6:11-13, 24; Rom. 5:1)
- **Jehovah-Tsidkenu**—"The Lord our Righteousness" (Jer. 23:6)
- **Jehovah-Ropheka** (or Ropha)—"The Lord our Healer" (Exo. 15:26)
- **Jehovah-Jireh**—"The Lord our Provider" (Gen. 22:14). The name Abraham gave God when He provided Abraham a ram to sacrifice. It also means "the Lord will help you see."
- **Jehovah-Nissi**—"The Lord our Banner" or "our victory" (Exo. 17:15). The name Moses gave God because of the victory over the Amalekites.
- **Jehovah-Tsabaoth**—"The Lord of Hosts" (1 Sam. 1:3; Isa. 47:4). God is our leader in battle and spiritual warfare. He is our authority. He has the right to give commands.
- **Jehovah-Meqaddeshkem**—"The Lord my Sanctifier" (Exo. 31:13). God is the God who cleanses and saves us.

Notice in the names of Jehovah that God is personally involved with our healing, our provision, our peace, etc. God was not a distant God in the Old Testament, as many would believe, including the people of Israel. God's intention has always been to be in intimate fellowship with His people. God's intention was to not only *be* significant in the lives of people but to impart His image, His significance *in* our lives for the purpose of relationship with others. The personal aspect of God was seen throughout the Old Testament through God's names and culminated ultimately in Jesus Christ. Jesus was also called "Emmanuel," which means "God *with* us." God's character is portrayed through His names and labels.

My prayer is that you open up your life to allow the Lord Jesus to be your significance. You are indeed significant to Him.

- God wants to be your most high God.
- God wants to be your strength and power.
- God wants to be the one who sees you and knows you (He already does).
- God wants to be your Master.
- God wants to be your Shepherd (to guide you and care for you).
- God wants to be your Peace.
- God wants to be your Righteousness.
- God wants to be your Healer.
- God wants to be your Sanctifier.
- God wants to be your Provider.
- God wants to be your Leader.
- God wants to be your Victory.

God is intimately interested in our lives. He loves us dearly and wants to provide us with our true identity in Him. God is significant, based on the many scriptural descriptions of His nature. He also sees us as significant to Him. Who *we* are starts with how *we* see the Lord *our* God.

Chapter 4
It All Starts with How We View God

And God said, "Who told you that you were naked?"
—Genesis 3:11

The Lord God, compassionate and gracious, slow to anger, and abounding in lovingkindness and truth; who keeps lovingkindness for thousands, who forgives iniquity, transgression, and sin; yet He will by no means leave the guilty unpunished.
Exodus 34:6-7

Who God is has been debated throughout the history of mankind. We often attempt to define God in our image, instead of defining ourselves in God's image. As a result, we perceive a much distorted God. "Through the history of the church, God's people have too often tended to zero in on a singular aspect of Him that served their purpose" (Stowell 2003, 24). If God is seen as only wrathful, we want to hide from Him. If God is seen as essentially distant, we believe He is disconnected from our lives and we are on our own. If God is seen as only loving, we believe anything goes, for after all, God will look the other way because He loves us. Each one of these views of God, by themselves, has led to heresy. These concepts provide only a partial description of the Almighty. How we view God affects how we see ourselves and how we conduct our lives. How we are defined completely hinges on the view we have of God.

The devil has been pretty successful in damaging our view of God through sin, disappointment, and pain. "Having parents who don't love us, spiritual leaders who disappoint us, or difficulties that we don't think we deserve often tempts us to invent a picture of God that is radically inconsistent with His true nature" (Stowell 2003, 24). Such experiences lead to a distortion of who God is. In turn, our own identity and significance is impeded. How we view God is critical in the discovery of who we are and where we are going.

Satan's Threefold Attack on God's Identity

Adam was the father of the human race. Scriptures make it clear that God had great plans for Adam and the rest of his offspring. Humans are created in God's image. Essentially, we all have been created in God's name and likeness. Ephesians 3:14-15 says, "For this reason I bow my knees before the Father, from whom *every* family in heaven and on earth *derives its name*" (emphasis added).

In the beginning we were loved and cared for by God the Father. We were to be fruitful and multiply upon the earth. We were to spread righteousness and God's principles upon the earth. We were to be responsible for God's creation on earth. We had open communication with God, completely without shame. "A world with no shame is pure paradise. It's a picture of heaven" (Wright 2005, 65). Pretty significant, don't you think?

However, our adversary, Satan, had other intentions. Satan's desire was to suggest God was not who He said He was, and that we were not who God said we were. "The beginning of all sin—the origin of all that is unloving—is a judgment about God" (Boyd 2007, 127). The devil was also determined to change our name! Unfortunately, he was successful in carrying out those intentions. He came into the garden of Eden and approached Adam and Eve and began a diabolical dialog with the first couple. As a result, nothing less than spiritual and natural devastation occurred.

Satan was able to place three primary doubts within the minds of Adam and Eve. First, the devil placed doubt about *God's Word*. The serpent asked, "Indeed, has God *said*, 'You shall not eat from any tree of the garden?'"(Gen. 3:1). Even though Eve responded by clarifying and singling out the only prohibited tree in God's command to them, the way Satan expressed the question initiated doubt toward the Word of God and the truth of God. This is the first thing the devil goes after—the *truth* of God or even the *truth* of anything.

Jesus clearly taught about Satan's true nature:

> "He was a murderer from the beginning, and does not stand in the truth because *there is no truth in him*. Whenever he speaks a lie, he speaks from his own nature, for he is a liar and the father of lies" (John 8:44, emphasis added).

God never said Adam and Eve could not eat from any tree of the garden.

> The Lord God commanded the man, saying, '*From any tree* of the garden you may *eat freely*; but from the tree of the knowledge of good and evil you shall not eat, for in the day that you eat from it you will surely die" (Gen. 2:16-17, emphasis added).

God was liberal in His provision toward Adam and Eve. They could eat from *any* tree *except* one. They had free reign on the earth, except for one boundary. That one boundary was set by God's intention of love and protection. However, Satan twisted that as well.

The second doubt Satan placed within Adam and Eve was regarding *God's intent*. The devil tried to suggest God was holding out on them. He said in Genesis 3:5, "For God knows that in the day you eat from it your eyes will be opened, and you will be like God, knowing good and evil." He was saying all they had to do was take for themselves and they would be better off than what God had done for them. This is the crux of the sinful nature and all of mankind's issues—for humans to believe we can obtain more than what God has provided and purposed and that truth is found through our own efforts without God. "The core of the lie that Adam and Eve believed was that they could be like God without God" (Benner 2004, 79).

An essential truth is that we are not God. Neither can we do for ourselves what the Lord can do for us. We are in His image, we are like Him, and we can reflect Him, as long as we stay surrendered to Him. Benner states:

> Paradoxically, Adam and Eve got what they wanted—to be like God without God, likeness that was based on independence rather than surrender . . . It is a lie because the autonomy that it promises is an illusion. We do not become free of God by a disregard of Divine will. Instead, by such disregard we forge the chains of our bondage" (Benner 2004, 80).

To be deceived into believing that we are something we are not, leads us to pursue meaning in our lives by our own means. If we leave God out of our self-discovery pursuits, we will find a distorted and unsatisfying self.

The devil has been successful in deceiving us into believing that only we have the power to achieve happiness in our own lives. "Everything that is false about us arises from our belief that our deepest happiness will come from living life our way, not God's way" (Benner 2001, 75). Fout adds, "The truth is that if anyone attempts to be absolutely self-determining and autonomous, and thus lordless, the result is inflicted pain and suffering on others and themselves" (Fout, 2011). No man can save himself or make himself righteous. Jesus came to provide salvation and healing in ways no man can ever provide.

Today I see signs that many people quickly assume and judge that others have bad intentions. We have become a cynical society, and as such, good intentions are ignored. I see children assume their parents have negative intentions. I see it existing in marital relationships toward each spouse. If a husband and wife are assuming his or her spouse has hurtful intentions, conflicts will arise. Authority figures are seen in a negative light more often than not. Realistically, some of it is deserved. However, much of it is not.

It is wrong to quickly assume evil intentions. Intentions come from the heart. Indeed, there are times evil intentions do exist, and I believe many people need discernment when such situations arise. However, we can be sure that if *good intentions* are always doubted, the devil is behind such thinking. If young people question the intentions of their parents, they often carry that into adulthood, and it affects their relationship with God and others.

Sometimes we may believe we are "helping" God. This is especially true if we believe God has revealed His plan for us. After all, if something is delayed or seems to be going against us, we'd better ignore the legitimate pitfalls and move "gung ho" forward.

Right? Just take and do for ourselves. That always works out for the best, doesn't it?

For example, Abraham and his wife, Sarah, perhaps believed they were helping God. After hearing God's promise to them of a son and seeing several years go by without seeing the fulfillment of the promise, they took it upon themselves to make it happen (Gen. 15-16). Impatience sometimes alters God's intentions toward our significance. God clearly promised a son to Abraham and Sarah. They may have felt and believed themselves to be overlooked or forgotten, thereby taking things into their own hands. Their false beliefs about their identity and God's intent eventually led them to do things they knew were not right.

Sarah, who was barren, suggested Abraham have sexual intercourse with her servant, Hagar, believing God would sanction the idea. After all, Sarah had not yet become pregnant, and there was a better chance a promised son would come from someone who was physically able to have a child. The result was Ishmael, who, as history reveals, became the link between Abraham and the Arab culture. Thirteen years later, Sarah gave birth to Isaac. He is the link between Abraham and the Jewish culture. World history has shown that the Middle East has been in conflict ever since. Often we make the mistake of asking God to sanction and bless something *we* are doing, rather than wait for the Lord to lead and provide, mostly because we doubt His intentions.

Jesus made some important statements to underscore the truth of God's intent toward us, which is to love us, to reveal Himself to us, to reveal who we are in Him, and to provide all we need. For example, John 15:15 says, "but I have called you friends, *for all things that I have heard from my Father I have made known to you*" (emphasis added). Jesus stated in John 14:1-2, "Do not let your heart be troubled; believe in God, believe also in me. In my Father's house are many dwelling places; *if it were not so, I would have told you*; for I go to prepare a place for you" (emphasis added). Finally, Jeremiah 29:11 presents God's intentions for us: "'For I know the plans that I have for you', declares the Lord, 'plans for welfare [*our well-being*] and not for calamity to give you a future and a hope.'"

God does not hide things *from* us; He often may hide things *for* us, for our best interest and for His higher purpose and good! Yet His intent is to give, not to withhold. In due time, according to His purpose and discretion, what God has for us He will give to us.

Perhaps the most diabolical part of this devilish lie was to doubt *who* God *is*. Over the centuries and throughout many cultures, God has been portrayed in many ways—usually in man's image. Today, the church is pretty good at helping us know *about* God. However, the church does not often succeed at helping us *know* God. Both are essential. One without the other leads to doctrinal imbalances and even heresy. One can know about God without being in relationship with Him. However, to know Him occurs only in relationship with Him. "If our purpose in life is to be like God, then we must know what He is like. How we perceive God directly determines how well we relate to Him and to those around us" (Stowell 2003, 24).

Seminaries, Bible schools, and churches teach much about doctrine and about God, and I have benefited from such resources. There are institutions that also allow for contemplation and the revelation of God, and I have experienced the impact in such settings. Together, my understanding of God and my relationship with God grew exponentially. But a person does not have to attend Bible school to be in relationship with God. The church is supposed to *encourage* relationship with God through instruction *and* experience. Knowing about someone is only part of the relationship. We need to experience the other person's presence to truly have a more intimate relationship. This is true in our relationship with God as well. He is a God who delights in revealing Himself to us. Benner states:

> Revelation is fundamental to the Divine character. God longs to disclose to us. Revelation is not simply something that happened at some distant point in the past. If it were, all we could ever hope for is information from this historic event (Benner 2004, 34).

God desires intimate relationship with men and women. Revelation of God is still possible today. Intimacy is experiential as well as informational. Jesus' life, death, and resurrection, and the sending of the Holy Spirit have provided ways for all of us to experience the true nature and presence of God.

God's revelation of His Divine character was one reason the devil was intent on preventing the coming of the Messiah and then to destroy Him when He did arrive on earth. The Bible is clear how the devil attempted to destroy the bloodline of the Messiah throughout Old Testament history. He continued the attempt in the New Testament as well. First the devil tried to kill the baby Jesus. Then Satan tried to destroy the adult Jesus several times in the gospel accounts (Matt. 2:13; Matt. 4:1-11; Matt. 12:14-16).

Jesus is the ultimate revelation of God. "Where else can you see His truth, grace, justice, holiness, righteousness, love, and mercy in such magnificent display?" (Stowell 2003, 25). Colossians 1:15 says, "He is the image of the invisible God." Also, Colossians 2:9 states, "In Him all the fullness of Deity dwells in bodily form."

We can know *about* God, but a relationship with Jesus, the name above all names, gives us the ability to experience Him. When God is diminished, the value of a man and a woman are diminished and human life is not sacred. Our identity and significance are also negatively impacted. When God is outright eliminated, the value of human life in general is lost. The more God is removed from a culture, the more chaos and evil will take place.

When people are wounded in life, they form distorted views and "names" for themselves. When a person feels lost, purposeless or disconnected, he or she will then attempt to find his or her name and identity through what the world offers. This is such a disastrous mistake! Doing so only reflects the sinful world, and such an identity is fleeting and unsatisfying. If we reflect a weak God in our lives, the result is self-centeredness. If we reflect no God in our lives, the result is emptiness, sin, and chaos. On the other hand, if we reflect God in our lives, there is glory to life. "When our picture of God is distorted, we can no longer trust God to be the source of our life" (Boyd 2007, 127). Mankind's true value is directly related to who we believe God is. "For he who comes to God must believe that He is and that He is a rewarder of those who seek Him" (Heb. 11:6). The following beliefs about God correlate to wrong approaches to life:

- God is distant or unreachable = people become self-pious, *hoping* God would take notice and accept them.
- God is withheld = people fall into self-power or self-sufficiency
- God is not concerned with us = people become self-centered

When we develop a wrong idea of God and ourselves, we develop a wrong idea of worship. It is through worship that we reflect the image of that which we worship.

Satan in the garden of Eden suggested to Adam and Eve that if they would just take from the forbidden tree, they would be like God, and as a result, be able to see God more clearly and to see as He sees. The truth was Adam and Eve *were already like God!* We would do well to remember that Satan has been a liar from the beginning—and he still is! Men and women were reflections of God, made in His image. They were also without sin and blemish. There was nothing more that Adam and Eve could have done, under their own power and efforts, to earn a higher standing in the eyes of God. Yet the devil was able to convince Adam and Eve that God was withholding from them and that they were deficient as a result. Both were lies. They belonged to Him and were like Him! He gave them all they needed. This was God's intent for all human beings. "The false self is the tragic result of trying to steal something from God that we did not have to steal" (Benner 2004, 80).

We were created in His image. We were created because of love, through love, and for love. We were given all we needed. We were placed in a role of significance. Jesus came to restore the relationship between God and man so we could once again represent Him. We were given a name, His name, to reflect and represent. There is no other name that is higher than the Lord Jesus Christ (Acts 4:12), and if we are related to Him by faith, we too have been redeemed and become defined by God once again. He placed such a tremendous value and significance upon humankind that He desired to redeem us to our rightful place as His sons and daughters. Isaiah 43:1 states, "Do not fear, for I have redeemed you; I have called you by name, you are Mine!"

The devil suggested that man could obtain a higher name and purpose through his own power and efforts—away from God. Once we leave the security and high standing that exists in relationship with the Lord, the devil is able to influence us with his lies. When Adam and Eve's "eyes were opened" (Gen. 3:7), they saw themselves instead of seeing God. When all we see is ourselves and our brokenness, we too will hide just like they did. Our significance takes a hit.

Of all the demonic influences that can occur against us, Foss suggests there are two essential roots from which the devil operates. "Written on these roots were their names. One was called insecurity, and the other was called inferiority" (Foss 2012, 6). We as human beings react to feelings of insecurity and inferiority in an attempt to reestablish our place in the world. Once the devil can define us through these powerful lies, we tend to seek whatever is available to help us feel secure and to feel significant. When our thirst for power exceeds our need to belong, to connect, or to experience real love, we then develop a kind of life that is full of drama and demands attention. The result is that we belong to outside influences or to ourselves, and not to God.

The truth is that whenever we attempt to become more than we are, essentially attempting to obtain our significance, we become less than who were created to be. Adam and Eve started this human trend. "*Instead, in trying to become God, they became less of themselves. And this is why we need spiritual growth. We have become less of what we were created to be*" (Cloud and Townsend 2001, 34). We become less empowered and more in bondage to something that inaccurately defines us. What appears to be self-made power becomes self-induced bondage. Benner says, "Truth is God himself who cannot be known apart from love and cannot be loved apart from surrender to His will" (Benner 2004, 35). If we see God for who He is, we can then understand how we are defined by Him. We are made by and called by *His* name. Only God's definition of who we are will ever bring true freedom, true purpose, and true empowerment.

Consider the story of the Tower of Babel. Not too long after the flood in Genesis had ended and the waters receded, mankind settled in the land of Shinar. The time was about three generations after Noah had disembarked from the ark onto dry land. Many of those people three generations later would have still remembered the story of the flood, especially since they were related to Noah and his sons. The intent of the hearts of those who built the tower is quite revealing. Genesis 11:4 says, "Come, let us *build for ourselves* a city, and a tower whose top will reach into heaven, and *let us make for ourselves a name*" (emphasis added). Through Noah, God delivered mankind from the evils of the world, yet it did not take long for mankind to attempt to redefine who they were. They tried to make a name for themselves, without God. They tried to become significant without God. They forgot that their name did not come from what they did to reach God but rather who God is and what God does to reach mankind!

Jesus in His great priestly prayer for His disciples prayed for each of these three aspects to be restored to the mind of any follower of Christ:

> Father, the hour has come; glorify Your Son, that the Son may glorify You . . . that *they may know You*, the only true God, and Jesus Christ, whom You have sent . . . I have manifested Your name to the men whom You gave me out of the world . . . now they have come to know that everything You have given Me is from You; for the words which You gave Me I have given to them . . . Holy Father, *keep them in Your name*, the name which You have given Me, that they may be one even as We are . . . Sanctify them in truth; Your *Word is truth*. (John 17:1-17, emphasis added)

Our identity is in Christ. We are created to reflect God. Only He has the power to correctly and properly define who we are. People, especially wounded people, usually have given others the power to define who they are. If we walk in the Lord's light and name, we are cherished indeed. Such knowledge of our name in the Lord can help us make better decisions, overcome evil, and be healed of our pain and woundedness.

Human beings were created to enjoy freedom, but not independence. Independence is doing as we please, answering to no one. The concept, while attractive, is not entirely possible. Freedom, on the other hand, is the *power* to do what is right and meaningful. Benner says, "Surrender is the foundational dynamic of Christian freedom—surrender of my efforts to live my life outside of the grasp of God's love and surrender to God's will and gracious Spirit" (Benner 2003, 60). Choosing to be independent from God, out from under God's covering, is disastrous for man. Brunner writes:

> The original source of all sin is the false independence of man over against God, the arrogance of his "equality," the falsity, the ingratitude and the pride of one who has forgotten that his life and all good depends absolutely on God, and can indeed only thus depend" (Brunner 1947, 72).

This independent thinking of man leads him down the path of foolishness, sin, alienation from God, confusion, addictions, disappointment, pain, and in reality, powerlessness. Essentially, as a result, man is left with a life that is less than what he had hoped and definitely less than what God designed. "Man's alienation from God at once carries with it his *self-alienation*" (Barth 1981, 213, emphasis added). Man can only find fulfillment in his life if he renounces and destroys his idols and becomes connected once again to God.

While we all need to deal with our own rebellion against God, through faith and devotion to Jesus Christ, many times we have been sinned against by others. The next chapter I will discuss how sin committed against us can cause distortions about God and ourselves.

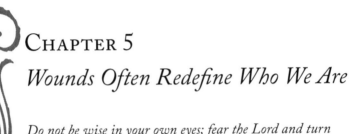

Chapter 5
Wounds Often Redefine Who We Are

Do not be wise in your own eyes; fear the Lord and turn away from evil. It will be healing to your body and refreshment to your bones.
Proverbs 3:7-8

I consider myself a late bloomer. I believed I was called into ministry when I was seventeen years old. However, it took many years and redirections and preparations before I was able to experience the fulfillment. I grew up in a mainline denominational church. I attended church often, had a good group of friends as a youngster and a teen, and had a healthy respect for God. I knew about Him, but I did not know Him.

Many things changed when my mother died of cancer. She was forty-nine years old. I was seventeen and a senior in high school. My dad chose to keep my brother and me in the dark about her real condition. However, at the moment she died, I experienced God for the first time. That may sound strange, but stay with me.

Created for Significance

At 5:50 a.m. on a Sunday morning, December 10, 1972, I woke up sensing someone gently shaking my shoulder while I slept. Upon waking, I saw no one in the room. I also found I could not go back to sleep, as I felt a peaceful presence filling the room. Within minutes of waking, our home phone rang and I heard my father's side of the conversation with the doctor. It went something like this: "Thank you, doctor, for letting me know . . . yes, I know you did all you could . . . thank you for all you did for my wife."

Then my father hung up. A couple more minutes went by, and in a tremoring voice, I heard my father call our pastor, asking if he could come over and "help me tell my boys that their mother just died." At that point I clearly sensed it was the presence of God who woke me so I could hear this conversation. Still sensing a peaceful presence that I just knew was the Lord, I asked in tears why he decided to wake me so I could hear that my mother had just died. To this day, I can quote His words verbatim: "Because I want to be a Father to you. I have set you apart for me." This experience carried me through my mother's wake, the funeral, and beyond.

Then, about two years later, returning home from a semester of college during Christmas break, I shared with my dad that I had decided to pursue the ministry. Even though he sent us to church, he did not have a relationship with the Lord at that time. Again, I can remember his words like it was yesterday: "Why don't you do something else? Something that would make the family proud." God's words to me early that morning of my mother's death, all of a sudden took a backseat to these words from my dad. While I had felt a sense of love, belonging, significance, and purpose from the Lord two years earlier, my dad's words caused that sense to go up in smoke for me. I know that should not have been true. I also know it should not have been true for Adam to believe anything except what

God said either, but he did. As a result, I was haunted by my father's words for years, and I struggled with purpose, significance, and fear of failure. It wasn't until I had several other encounters with God over the last twenty years, including a few during seminary studies for my doctor of ministry degree, that He gradually empowered me with His words, purpose, and significance once again.

God's presence and His words defined me that morning in December 1972. My dad's words about two years later also defined me—or more accurately redefined me for many years. The ironic thing was that I did not fail too often in what I placed my effort toward. Yet the fear of failure, fear of what others thought of me, and lack of a sense of significance and purpose continued to hamper me. I carried myself in such a way that I often chose to shrink back. In the movie, "Home Run", produced by Hero Productions and Impact Productions (2013), the main character Cory Brand spoke to one of his little league baseball players: "Nothing good happens when you hold back." He is right. The Lord's renewing presence in my life has lifted me to see things differently and to experience His affirmations in me. For the last several years I have been experiencing the ability to carry myself in His name, by His grace, and through His power. Knowing I am His, *really* knowing I am His has helped me better understand and experience His rest while He meets my core longings. It is never too late—for anyone!

Among my clients and students, I usually give homework assignments to write essays, two of which are titled "How Did I Get the Way That I Am?" and "What Is Most Important to Me?" They are designed to cause reflection about who they are, which often determines where they are going. The following are some excerpts of these essays, providing a glimpse of the importance of identity-forming in individuals.

One person wrote, "My mom has never been supportive of me or my dreams. In fact, she has always called me dumb and a dipstick, which hurt my feelings."

A young woman who grew up in a broken home wrote, "My daughter defines who I am. Someone on this earth loves me for me and needs me; that is important to me. I have someone to care for and provide for." Notice how this person is expressing at least four of the human core longings: love, understanding, purpose, and significance.

Another person wrote,

> Unfortunately, I wasn't told that in life being free to be who I am wasn't a bad thing. I thought that I had to please people. So much time and energy went into sulking, being down, lying in bed, and crying.

This individual struggled with depression because she had not discovered who she was, nor did she receive the encouragement to discover and pursue her dreams.

A women wrote,

> When I was a young child, I don't recall ever being hugged or told 'I love you.' I never had a birthday party until I was twenty-six years old. On my thirteenth birthday I was helping my mother and stepdad rake the yard. No one had so much as mentioned that it was my birthday, so I kindly told my mother that it was my birthday. She said, 'Okay, it's your birthday, now get to work.' I was crushed by her comment. From that day forward, my self-concept was that I was worthless and didn't mean very much to anyone or the world. I am thirty-nine years old and I am still lost, still trying to find out who I am and why I am here.

A man wrote, "Growing up was a big problem for me. I was a little overweight . . . and then everyday hearing 'you're fat' or 'dough boy' made me feel worthless and not value myself for who I really was as a person."

One young man who worked in both law enforcement and as a resource officer in the public schools wrote, "I've seen what can happen when a child grows up without parents who care for them . . . running with gangs and then stumble into school late, without being fed, and looking like a mess." He later admitted that by witnessing such young people, he learned to love his own children in a sincere way. Love, feeling significant, and feeling a sense of belonging have a tremendous affect on who we are and what we do.

Betty

I also give other types of homework to individuals and couples I counsel, and writing letters to others and to God are some common assignments. Betty (not her real name) came to counseling at first because of reported marriage issues at first. A thirty-year-old woman with one middle-school-age child, she appeared anxious, had trouble staying on topic, and felt her husband would never change. As we spent weekly sessions together, I discovered Betty had a little secret—she had been trying to hide a prescription pill addiction from her family. When her addiction was out in the light, we began to focus on her addiction, her painful early life, and her ownership of dealing with her woundedness. We began to focus on where she obtained her identity. Listen to a letter from Betty as she writes to and about her mother:

> Well, when I was a little girl she really never took care of me. But she always had my father beat us black and blue. She always was sleeping around on my dad and had

us with her. I always felt like I didn't belong because the only thing I was any good at was being put in the middle of their fights or getting beat all the time. So finally I got put into foster care. She says she tried to fight to get us back but she wouldn't leave her child-molesting husband to get me back. So I had to stay in foster care. She never gave me a mother-daughter bond. Because if it's not about her or something in it for her then she doesn't know you or want anything to do with you. She has always put me on the back burner for everyone else because they had all the material things. But all I ever asked her for was her love as a mother because I never knew how a mother's love felt.

Betty is expressing at least three core longings (if not all six): *love, safety, and belonging*. Because of sin and neglect toward Betty, she did not experience the sense of belonging she desired and the sense of love for her young life. As she grew into an adult, the pain that occurred because they were missing led her into a life of depression and addiction to prescription drugs that almost destroyed her marriage and almost killed her. She also experienced abuse and a rape while in foster care, which greatly impacted her.

Betty was encouraged to attend Alcoholics Anonymous (AA) and Narcotics Anonymous (NA), in concert with our counseling sessions, which she did faithfully for many months. After a short time, she shared with me how much she felt so quickly accepted by others who were in the programs (belonging). She was gratified that those who were there were very much like her (understanding). Betty also felt excited to have something to do every day, when she attended her meetings, instead of being depressed at home, watching TV all the time, and "zoning out" (purpose). Finally, between our counseling sessions and the AA or NA meetings, she grew comfortable sharing about her hurts and hopes (safety).

She had a simple, child-like faith, and we began to speak a lot about Jesus and His experience on Earth. She eventually allowed me permission to pray for and with her after every counseling session. After a couple of months, I asked Betty to write a letter to God. Here is what she wrote:

> Well God, I don't know where to begin. But I do need your hands laid upon me. I am going through so much and you know and you also know my heart. You know what's going on with my marriage. God, you know everything. I know you are only one God, but God, I need you so bad. God, I can't do nothing without you. God, why is it that my pain, anger, and resentment to a lot of people I can't let go? I have always acted like I'm ok. But I'm not, God. You have saved my life so many times. What is my purpose for being here on earth? God, please guide and show me. Because it hurts when I walk around everyday feeling like no one loves or cares about me. They put on the act that they love me and care but for some reason my heart doesn't feel this way. God, I'm crying out to you for your power, will, hope, strength. And I'm crying for you to show me my purpose. These things I ask in your powerful name. Amen.

Betty's sweet, heartfelt letter opened her up for further healing and restoration. Her core longings for love and purpose especially stand out. It was wonderful to watch the Lord do a deliberate work of loving on this dear woman.

Betty believed her "names" were "thrown away"; "overlooked"; "unloved"; "addict"; "dumb"; and "good for nothing." She never did finish high school and as an adult believed she was not very smart. As we spent time in counseling, she learned she was indeed bright and very discerning. She simply had no one else in her life who could believe and declare that these things were true. Over time and through inner healing by the Holy Spirit, Betty was able to have a voice in her marriage, overcome her pill addiction, and eventually began to grow in her self-esteem. One present goal is to now complete her GED.

Mike

Mike was raised in a strict and abusive home. He reported that he was not encouraged or affirmed in anything he did. He barely made it through high school. Mike, now in his mid-fifties, was a talented guy, but he had a tremendous amount of difficulty rising to the occasion and using his talents in a confident manner. He also grew up going to church and being active in the choir as an adult. He and his wife enjoyed music, and each had a good singing voice, but his lack of confidence compelled him to quit the choir. He would eventually join the choir again, only to quit again.

One day, Mike was laid off his job after more than twenty years with the company. He was devastated. His wife remained encouraging, but he quickly fell into a deep depression. He became isolated from friends and church and once again quit the choir. This time he wrote a letter to the church leadership indicating his disappointment with God and his decision to quit the choir:

> I feel He has deserted me and there is no hope. I have no purpose in life. Without a purpose, what are you? I consider myself to be a failure and not because I wanted to be. I wish I felt good about myself but nevertheless I don't. I don't understand God at all. I have lost faith in God and don't know who I am anymore. I don't live now, I just exist. Instead of becoming better, I find myself becoming bitter. I don't feel like singing now because I have no song in my heart. I have no joy or peace. My burden is heavy. Sometimes I'm tired of life. . . . I'm no good to myself, family or others.

Then Mike signed it, "A shell of a man; Mr. Failure." Mike sounds like a broken man. In his short attempt in counseling, he reported that he had several job offers, but he just could not accept any of them. His depression caused him to be immobilized. Notice how his faith in God was directly related to who he was. Once he lost dependency upon God, he lost himself. He was not able or willing to do the difficult but freeing work of counseling through inner healing prayer.

Unfortunately, Mike did not return to counseling, and he and his wife eventually divorced. While his wife remains in church, Mike has not. He is currently working but is underemployed. He is currently living with a family member and we have lost touch.

Trudy

Another woman in her early thirties, who I will call Trudy, came to counseling. She was depressed and had an alcohol addiction. She was a young married mother of three and gave the appearance that all was pretty good in her life and home. The truth was she had an alcohol problem that only her husband knew about and it was the cause of great conflict. As she began counseling, she shared about her upbringing and the "names" she developed for herself.

Trudy's mother was a single mother who'd had many men come and go in and out of their home. Her mother was also an alcoholic. As a youngster, Trudy often heard from her mother that she was not wanted, that her mom wished she'd had an abortion, and that giving birth to Trudy had ruined her life. She also witnessed selfishness as her mother tended to her own needs over Trudy's. Trudy considered suicide several times in her life. Trudy's "names" were "unwanted"; "overlooked"; "unlovable"; "unimportant"; and "addict," and she felt like her life was not valid.

As we progressed through counseling, she began to respond to seeing her life as God saw her. She even began attending AA meetings, but she was not consistent in her attendance and would hang out with other struggling addicts away from the meetings and continued drinking. When she admitted these struggles to me, we devised a drastic plan, with which her husband agreed. With family encouragement and support, Trudy agreed to admit herself to Teen Challenge, a residential Christ-centered drug and alcohol rehab program designed for individuals from ages eighteen to about fifty. Even though she had to travel to another state for residential treatment, which lasted a year, she stayed with the program. Her husband continued to be supportive, and their extended family and local church supported him to help with childcare, emotional support, and spiritual support when needed.

Trudy's life and identity completely changed as she increasingly learned that Jesus loved her, and she was able to experience such love. As she approached the end of her treatment, she shared that she felt she would have a significant purpose for helping other addicts in their struggles.

When she returned home, she and her husband continued attending counseling for a couple of months. Trudy expressed how she saw her life return to her, how she became defined by God, and how free she felt for the first time. Her desire to help and minister to others opened doors for her to share with women's groups about addictions and lead her into the expressive dance ministry at her church. Today, Trudy continues in her freedom and enjoys her life with her sons and husband.

Robert B. Shaw, Jr.

Terry

When Terry was a young boy, he believed he had a perfect family. He was the older of two brothers, and his mom and dad were married. He was athletic and bright. One day, during dinnertime, his parents shook his world when they told him and his brother they were getting divorced. He was eleven years old at the time.

For several weeks Terry frantically tried to be a peacemaker and keep his family together. Terry's father eventually left, and his parents completed their divorce. From that point on Terry believed he had failed. His life then became one of dipping grades, moving from school to school between living with his mom and then for a time with his dad, and then back with his mom and new stepfather. In between these years, he tried to referee fights between his mother and a boyfriend. The boyfriend was physically abusive to his mother, and Terry felt powerless to do anything about it. Even though that relationship in his mother's life eventually ended, Terry again felt a sense of failure—failure to stop the abuse and protect his mother.

Terry grew to believe he was a failure. He became quiet and introspective and had few friends. Even though he was a good, university-level athlete, his athletic career was one of frustration as coaches would either overlook him or be hard on him when he made mistakes. These experiences continued to feed his belief that he was a failure.

Terry also experienced relationship issues. He had a girlfriend in high school and early college who eventually broke up with him. He had difficulty with his stepfather, his biological dad, and his mother, who became an alcoholic. He had one marriage that ended in divorce, was laid off from two jobs, and experienced heartbreaking miscarriages. His first wife and current wife were not able to carry children to term. Terry never was able to experience being a father.

All of these experiences continued to underscore his belief that Terry was a failure in all areas of his life.

When Terry came to counseling, he was in his early fifties. He was deeply depressed and had loud, angry episodes, especially with his wife. Whenever he made a mistake, even the smallest of mistakes, he would overreact and explode in anger because, after all, he was a failure, and he hated himself. He had few meaningful relationships since he believed no one would really want to spend time with a failure.

I asked Terry to complete a "loss timeline," and he listed twenty-six "losses" that he experienced—most of which he classified as directly his fault, which of course was not the case. Among the things he listed were, his family; his home; and his confidence. He had such a vivid memory of all these experiences, it was as if he was still reliving them.

We would discuss his life, and after some time we were able to discover that Terry had many experiences that were successful and positive, yet he could not see them that way. We spent a lot of time reviewing his life and positioning him to experience the love and acceptance of Jesus. Terry attended church, but more out of habit and obligation than true relationship with God.

As time went on, Terry slowly began to understand he was not responsible for his parents' divorce; that as a child, it was not his responsibility to keep his family together; that the miscarriages were not his fault; that the loss of his jobs were not because of his performance; and that his life was not just filled with failures. He was a well-respected and dependable professional who chose to work with integrity. He felt deeply about doing the right thing. He had attended a famous and prestigious university on an academic scholarship. His current wife was a good woman who loved him. Finally, he was experiencing the love of God through the Holy Spirit moving upon his life. God was slowly redefining Terry's life and outlook. Terry was slowly feeling more confident, less impatient, and less like a failure. The bottom line for Terry was that he did not fail others as much as others failed him.

The Holy Spirit began to restore Terry's heart, and he learned forgiveness was possible—for others in his life and for himself. We journeyed through the process of forgiveness. First he identified his inner pain and how the offenses and emotional wounds defined him. Then he learned how to release the many individuals who hurt him. We also dealt with self-loathing, and Terry began to feel a release within his own spirit. His relationship with God was developing in a deeper way, and his marriage began to improve. He was seeing more clearly how much his wife loved him and how she had supported him over the years. He was becoming more attentive to her, more patient and understanding. Now in his early fifties, he even participated in a competitive sport and felt some fulfillment in it.

God continues to redefine Terry's life not as a failure but as someone who is loved and can live in grace, even when things do not always go as planned. We will all fail, but that does not make us a failure. While the reversal of consequences is not always possible, a substantial level of recovery can be possible. Terry learned that the Lord is still in the redeeming business, and his own identity can take on a new meaning.

Carlie

Carlie had a beginning that has become quite common. She came to counseling as an eighteen-year-old young lady. Her parents were still teenagers when she was conceived. They were married just a couple of months before Carlie was born. She reported that while she was growing up, her mom and dad constantly argued and were verbally abusive toward each other. They were also very strict with her, seemingly controlling her every move. She often heard her parents argue that their marriage was a mistake and having Carlie was a mistake. Carlie developed the name "mistake" as her young life developed. She also felt "unwanted." After all, her parents' lives would not have been ruined and so miserable had it not been for her coming along, right? That is what she believed.

As a result of her life being a mistake in her own mind, Carlie began to make many mistakes through the choices she was making. She began to crave attention, so her attractive appearance became her focus, and she gained much attention as a result. Yet she was still in turmoil. She became a cutter, which is someone who uses sharp objects to make cuts on their bodies, as a way to release anger and pain. She also often had suicidal thoughts and attempted suicide twice, prior to coming to counseling. Her mom was prescribed antidepressants, and Carlie would steal her mother's pills in order to get high. She was not completing her homework and cheated on tests in order to pass her classes in high school. She also hung around other young people who were bad influences on her life. Carlie would break rules, break curfews, and skip classes. Finally, Carlie admitted to being a habitual liar, mostly to her parents, but also to others in her life. It was at this point that Carlie's mom brought to counseling. After several sessions, Carlie expressed a desire to learn why she chose to lie so much. Carlie had to discover that her life itself was not a lie or a mistake!

As we spent time in counseling sessions together, Carlie began to realize that her identity as a "mistake" drove her to try just about anything to find out who she was. It wasn't until she realized God gave her a real life with a purpose that her perspective began to change. She is discovering she had real dreams but never thought she could achieve them. She is discovering that she belonged to God first, and that He loves her. She is slowly opening her life to the Holy Spirit and is beginning to see a transformation of her identity. While her teenaged parents may not have planned for her, Carlie is gradually understanding that her life was precious and purposeful. The Lord is slowly establishing a new identity and a new sense of character and integrity for Carlie. She is learning to choose better behaviors that provide better outcomes than she had experienced in the past.

Some of her relationships still need to change as they are negative, albeit familiar influences in her life. Carlie is slowly learning that many of her friends helped define who she believed she is. That piece is still in process. One main positive thing Carlie is doing: as of this writing, she has begun to pursue her dream of becoming a nurse and has enrolled in college.

Stephen

The following is a written testimony that came from a twenty-five-year-old young man, who I will call Stephen, as he described a period of his life during his late teens:

> One day I came home from spending the night out and my father was gone. My mom sat down with me and my sister and told us that she and dad were not together anymore. Keep in mind that I never saw my parents fight or speak ill of each other. This had a devastating effect on me. At this point in my life I began to rebel against everything my parents taught me. I started drinking and smoking marijuana and cigarettes . . . it seemed that everyone was doing these things and that it was just harmless fun. I was very active physically but began to notice a pain in my hip joint during my freshman year at college. I went to the doctor for X-rays. Arthritis had completely taken over my left hip joint. He prescribed pain medicine . . . and this was the beginning of the end

Created for Significance

> for me. I thought opiates were a miracle drug. They killed my physical pain and also soothed the emotional anguish I had deep inside of me.

This young man eventually developed an opiate addiction, along with an alcohol addiction by the age of twenty-three. He had begun to believe certain things about himself that flipped the labels of who he was. His security changed, and Stephen decided to seek the answers for security and peace in places that led him away from the very things he was seeking. Within the next three years, Stephen got married, introduced his wife to a life of substance abuse, had a child, was in an automobile accident, and robbed a bank to help support their substance dependency. He was later caught and landed in jail.

While Stephen was in jail, his testimony began to change. He wrote:

> This was the lowest point of my life, and when I thought I wanted to end it all I cried out to Jesus. I started asking Him questions like, 'How did my life ever get to this point?' And He answered, 'You were living your life based on lies.' I then realized that I based my life on the idea that life was meaningless, that everything was eventually doomed for failure so why try, and that there was no purpose for my existence.

Notice how Stephen identified his life as "meaningless," with "no purpose," "a failure," and based on "lies." Once Stephen began to believe the lies about his identity and life, his behaviors changed and his life went spiraling downward.

It was soon after Stephen found himself in jail that he petitioned the judge during the pretrial period to allow him to go to a Christian-based rehab center for his addictions. Surprisingly, the judge granted Stephen's request. This action was unprecedented in the local courts at the time. This is when I met Stephen. He became part of a small counseling group that I was conducting with other addicts. He was twenty-six years old at the time.

After spending many weeks together during our inner healing prayer small group, this has become Stephen's ongoing testimony:

> Jesus began to deliver me from these lies. He told me that I was a child of God and that He created me for a specific purpose. He said He loved me so much that He died on the cross for me so I could live a victorious life with abundant blessings, that I was sacred in His eyes, and that my body was a holy temple to be revered and cared for with the utmost reverence. As He began to incorporate these truths into my life, I noticed that my whole mentality changed. He loved me so much that he brought me to my knees so that I would call to Him and pray to Him and He would listen to me. He made himself real to me.

Stephen truly benefited from his time at the Christian rehab center and experienced the Lord during our small group. He has since completed his rehab, knowing God is with him every moment. At the time of this writing, Stephen is back in jail serving his final sentence as the consequence of his behaviors. For a time I continued corresponding with Stephen, and he remains a changed man, depending on Jesus, and hopeful that he can return home soon. While he knows he has to serve several years in prison, Stephen has placed his life in God's hands and has developed a new identity based on the love and purpose of God in his life.

Here is an excerpt from a personal letter he sent me from jail several months after our small group concluded:

> I also want to thank you for the group you conducted. It had a lasting impact on my life. When I look back at it now, it is in gratitude for the cleansing effect it had on my

past conceptions of myself. The activity that effected me the most was when you had us wipe off of our faces and from our life a past lie that was formerly adhered to. For me it was the lie that "anything I do would fail, so why try?" Your group, along with a combination of many other positive forces, contributed to my newfound motivation and belief that I am not a failure and that I can expend my energies towards positive endeavors, and that they will be beneficial to me and others.

Stephen was referring to an encounter with the Lord through a symbolic yet powerful approach that is a small part of Healing Care Group materials designed by Dr. Terry Wardle, and that I use with others in counseling. Other ways to help find your identity and significance will be discussed in the last chapter.

These individuals are just a few examples of how one's identity can be impacted as a result of hurt, pain, disappointment, and consequences of negative behavior. When people realize their identity and significance has been negatively affected, it is important that we come to Jesus and begin to be identified with Him and to be called by His name.

The next chapter will present several biblical characters that we may be able to relate to as well, and we will see how God was able to restore their true identities.

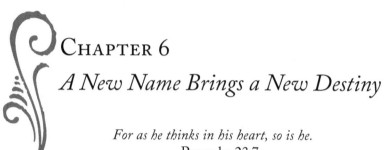

Chapter 6

A New Name Brings a New Destiny

For as he thinks in his heart, so is he.
—Proverbs 23:7

Being true to who we are in Christ and remaining consistent to our life in His name can be difficult in times of temptation, discouragement, woundedness, stress, and desperation. During these times, it is critical to stay connected to God, our source of life, so as to not deviate from our identity. This can be described as integrity. Integrity can be defined as being the same person when no one is looking as when others are watching. Jesus is an excellent example of such integrity. Of course the argument can be made that He was Divine and God in the flesh. This is true. However, Peter, Mephibosheth, and Joseph of the Old Testament are also excellent examples. They are perhaps more realistic models for us. Joseph's integrity of his identity remained true. In Peter's and Mephibosheth's case, their integrity of their identity either was developed or restored. Despite their disappointments, victimization, false accusations, and discouragement, they eventually experienced God's redeeming power and influence to redefine their significance.

Peter

Let's begin with Peter. Jesus first met Andrew, Peter's brother, and apparently Andrew believed Jesus to be the Messiah (John 1:40-42). Andrew then spoke about Jesus to Peter, and when Jesus came by the fishing boats, Andrew introduced Peter to Jesus. They were fishing at the time, and when Jesus called them both to be "fishers of men," they left their nets and immediately followed Jesus (Matt. 4:18; Mark 1:18). Peter was quick to act, and in this case, that was appropriate. In other instances, his impulsiveness and fear got him into trouble.

As we discussed in Chapter 3, Peter's name, which means "rock," was changed from Simon ("little stone"). Perhaps he lived his life by other names like "fear" and "impulsiveness." When Jesus invited him to take a walk on the water (Matt. 14:22-33), he did so, but fear overtook him. Once he took his eyes off Jesus and became aware of his own inability, he sank. Then, there is Peter's denial of Christ (John 18:15-27). Out of fear once again, he denied knowing Christ in order to save himself from arrest and harm.

The same is true for us. We cannot rely on just our own abilities, because if we do, we will falter, sink, and run as well. If we walk in *His* name and according to *His* word, we will eventually see positive outcomes.

Peter also showed his impulsiveness when Jesus was about to wash the disciples' feet (John 13). Peter refused to allow Jesus to do so but instead implored Him to wash his hands and head. He also showed his impulsiveness when he drew a sword to try to defend Jesus at the time of His arrest, cutting off the servant's ear (John 18:10).

Finally, Peter was nowhere to be found during Jesus' trial and crucifixion. John was the only disciple who was at the cross. Peter went back to being a "fisher of fish," his old name and identity, perhaps to find familiarity and fulfillment after so much upheaval and disappointment. Peter reverted back to his past life and identity once again.

Disappointments and weariness will often do that—tempt us to return to the old and familiar ways that we developed for ourselves, instead of living in the new identity Jesus provides. By doing so, we rob ourselves of our true significance being a new person in Christ.

Jesus, however, made no mistake in renaming Peter from "little stone" to "rock." After Jesus' resurrection, the angel sitting in the tomb made sure the women who came to the empty tomb would specifically seek out Peter to tell him of the resurrection (Mark 16:7). Then, after Jesus appeared to His disciples, He questioned Peter three times about his love for the Lord (John 21:15-17). Jesus knew of Peter's impulsiveness to respond too quickly. Perhaps that is why He patiently asked Peter several times, so Peter would realize the importance of his responses.

It is critical that we not only learn our new name and identity but we learn to embrace and tenaciously hold on to it. Do not let disappointment or fear—or someone else—steal your identity or name. Do not let situations and others rob your significance. Our love of God, and the conviction of His love for us, determines whether we will persevere in our new name and identity despite the challenges that will come. Jesus was teaching Peter that what was yet to come in his future—namely his effectiveness in his preaching and ministry as well as his own martyrdom and crucifixion (John 21:19)—would be for the glory of God.

A careful reader only has to read the book of Acts and the Epistles that Peter had written to see the transformation of a fearful and impulsive man to a steadfast and mighty man of God. Simon had to "die" in order for Peter to have "life." Jesus changed his name from "Simon" to "Peter" because of his future! He was not to remain a fisher of fish; Jesus saw him in the future as a fisher of men.

Acts 2, for example, reports the experience of the empowerment of the Holy Spirit at Pentecost upon the disciples. In Acts 2:14-41 we read Peter's first sermon, and the three thousand converts that resulted. Not bad for a fearful and impulsive man who began as a fisher of fish. God's intended identity for us can also be fruitful and fulfilling as well, in many situations and to varying degrees.

Benner observes the new knowledge Peter gained about God and himself in just the first Epistle of Peter alone:

- God is the source of new life and living hope that is based in the resurrected Christ (1 Peter 1:3).
- God is the source of a faith that is more precious than gold (1 Peter 1:7).
- God is a fountain of inexpressible joy (1 Peter 1:8).
- God judges with fairness and impartiality (1 Peter 1:17).
- God allows us to share Christ's sufferings as a way of knowing Jesus through identification (1 Peter 4:12-13).
- God is faithful and can be trusted to do what is right (1 Peter 4:19).
- God is opposed to the proud but gives grace to the humble (1 Peter 5:6). (Benner 2004, 36-37)

Peter never denied his Lord again. He became a pillar of the early Christian Church, and history showed that he was indeed crucified for his faith. Peter, in fact, chose to be crucified upside down because he did not feel worthy of being crucified in the same manner as Jesus (Winston 1926, 4).

Mephibosheth

Mephibosheth was a young man who experienced a dramatic transformation of his name and identity. He was a son of Jonathan, who was a close friend to David prior to David becoming king of Israel. King Saul, who had attempted to kill David more than once, was Jonathan's father and Mephibosheth's grandfather. In other words, Mephibosheth was royalty and had a grand destiny.

In 2 Samuel 4:4 we are introduced to Mephibosheth as a young boy:

> Now Jonathan, Saul's son, had a son crippled in his feet. He was five years old when the report of Saul and Jonathan came from Jezreel, and his nurse took him up and fled. And it happened that in her hurry to flee, he fell and became lame. And his name was Mephibosheth.

Mephibosheth was five years old when the Philistines killed his father and grandfather. He was in the care of a nurse who, in her haste to run from the advancing Philistines, picked up Mephibosheth and ran. The actual Hebrew language in the above passage can be rendered that she *dropped* him, and as a result, he became crippled. This young boy, who was the grandson of the king, lost both his grandfather and father in battle and became crippled due to an accident. Family tragedy and a debilitating accident changed Mephibosheth's identity and destiny, or so it seemed.

Later, in 2 Samuel chapter 9, Mephibosheth reappears. This time, David is now king of Israel, and he is seeking to bless anyone who may be left in his friend Jonathan's family. He sends for a servant in the house of Saul named Ziba, who reports to David that, "There is still a son of Jonathan who is crippled in both feet" (2 Sam. 9:3). Notice how Mephibosheth is named and identified—as a cripple, not as a prince! Ziba continues his report, describing that Mephibosheth is now a member of the house of Machir in the city of Lo-Debar (2 Sam. 9:4-5). The name Machir means "a merchant," or "to sell." In other words, Mephibosheth was apparently a lowly servant living in a merchant's home. He could not have been very highly valued being he was crippled and limited in his ability to produce in the home of a merchant. Also, the name of the city of Lo-Debar adds to Mephibosheth's identity. Lo-Debar in Hebrew means "pastureless"; "of no significance"; "of no regard." He was living a lowly, insignificant life far from what he was originally destined to be. As we shall see, he believed these labels to be his identity.

However, King David had something else in mind. The king sends for Mephibosheth and 2 Samuel 9:6-7 describes what transpires:

> Mephibosheth, the son of Jonathan the son of Saul, came to David and fell on his face and prostrated himself. And David said, "Mephibosheth." And he said, "Here is your servant!" David said to him, "Do not fear, for I will surely show kindness to you for the sake of your father Jonathan, and will restore to you all the land of your grandfather Saul; and you shall eat at my table regularly."

Incidentally, Mephibosheth's name means "dispeller of shame," or "to drive away shame." David called Mephibosheth by his given name, as if to say, "Your shame will indeed be driven away!" David called Mephibosheth's by his true identity and declared his significance. David also intended to restore his inheritance and identity as royalty by making sure the lad regularly dined with the king.

However, listen to Mephibosheth's response. While he was indeed respectful to the king, his discouraging circumstances and negative self-talk produced disparaging comments. Jesus said, "But the things that proceed out of the mouth come from the heart" (Matt. 15:18). 2 Samuel 9:8 reads, "Again he prostrated himself and said, 'What is your servant, that you should regard a dead dog like me?'" He was devalued, depressed, and disabled, yet the king brought royalty back to his life. The king ordered Ziba and his servants to serve Mephibosheth and to be sure his inheritance and affairs were to be properly maintained. Even though Mephibosheth was crippled, he would be cared for with honor and dignity.

Second Samuel 9:7, 10, 11, and 13 repeated that Mephibosheth would be dining with the king regularly, as one of the king's sons. Mephibosheth truly experienced a fulfillment of his name, whereby shame was ultimately driven from him. By virtue of our king, Jesus, we can also have our rightful place with the king restored and be identified by His name! We may be "crippled" by our sin or by sin committed against us, but Jesus has restoration in mind for all of us! "There is no longer a need to strive, grab, please people, or compete in order to find a place at the table. Our identity as God's beloved is all we will ever need" (Wardle 2004, 38).

Joseph

The story of Joseph begins in Genesis chapter 37. Joseph was one of the twelve sons of Jacob, or Israel. His life is an excellent example of how others tried to ruin and distort his identity and significance. There are at least four contrasting identities that Joseph had to wrestle with. Was Joseph

- Spoiled or favored?

- Dreamer or prophet?
- Overpowered or overcomer?
- Overlooked or held over?

Spoiled or Favored

In Genesis 37:2, seventeen-year-old Joseph is found to have brought back a bad report to his father regarding his brothers and the way they apparently were conducting themselves while shepherding their father's flocks. Even as a youth, Joseph showed early signs of integrity and a desire to do what is right. Such a description of Joseph will remain consistent as his story unfolds in Genesis.

Verse 3 makes it clear that Israel loved Joseph more than all his brothers. Some may claim that Joseph was spoiled. Some may claim he was favored. Which identity is correct? I believe Joseph was favored. There is an important difference between spoiled and favored. According to the dictionary, to spoil means "to do harm to the character of, by overindulgence or excessive praise." Also, it means "to rob." In your consideration, think about a spoiled child that you might know. That child has been robbed of responsibility and the ability to live in a realistic world. I have counseled several parents and their children, who were spoiled, and these youngsters have a spirit of entitlement. I have found this in some adults as well, who were coddled and spoiled as children and teenagers.

It is true that Israel did make a multicolored tunic for only Joseph and not for his other sons. However, Joseph was not exempt from his father's criticism. When Joseph later shared one of his dreams with his father, his father rebuked and even ridiculed him (Gen. 37:10). As a result, it did not seem as if Joseph always got a free pass. Joseph's ability to live with integrity and good character came from at least three sources: he apparently knew his standing with his father; he was secure in his relationship with his father; and he lived by righteous standards.

Favor, on the other hand, is defined in the dictionary as "a token of special regard for, or approval of," or "to bless." Israel indeed had a special regard for Joseph, and he sought to bless him with the multicolored tunic. Some may say favor can be synonymous with grace or mercy. Scriptures often use the words mercy, grace, and favor. They are different words with different concepts.

Mercy is when love is given to those *who cannot deserve it*, as with people who have no way of obtaining what they need. When I think of mercy, I think of the late Mother Teresa of Calcutta. Her organization was called "Sisters of Mercy." She cared for children who were orphans and throwaway children. They surely could not obtain what they needed without her help.

Grace is love given to those *who do not deserve it*. For example, human beings are saved by grace. We walk in iniquity and sin, "But God demonstrated His own love toward us, in that while we were yet sinners, Christ died for us" (Rom. 5:8). We do not deserve pardon from our iniquity, but we received forgiveness because of Christ's death on the cross and resurrection. Through Christ, our standing before God is a gift that we do not deserve, but God desired to give because of His love for us.

Favor is not the same as grace. Favor, in the Greek language is *charis*, which means "graciousness." In other words, favor is the *living out and the manifestation of the power of grace* in someone's life. Proverbs 11:27 says, "He who diligently seeks good seeks favor, but he who seeks evil, evil will come to him." Favor is seen in someone who walks in humility. Such an individual knows that everything he or she possesses ultimately has been bestowed upon him or her.

For example, Jehoshaphat was shown favor because he ruled as a righteous king of Judah:

> The Lord was with Jehoshaphat because he followed the example of his father, David's, earlier days and did not seek the Baals, but sought the God of his father, followed His commandments, and did not act as Israel did. So the Lord established the kingdom in his control, and all Judah brought tribute to Jehoshaphat, and he had great riches and honor (2 Chron. 17:3-5).

Also, favor can be given to someone who walks in grace and righteousness. Vine says, "Grace is a free gift; favor may be deserved or gained" (Vine 1985, 229). I believe it is more accurate to understand favor as gained, as a consequence of a righteous, humble, and honorable lifestyle.

Joseph had favor in his father's heart as a result of his desire to do the right thing and walk in integrity. When one carries himself with integrity and dependability, favor is often given. The result of submission to God is a life that increasingly reflects Him. The apostle Paul describes the fruit of the Spirit in Galatians 5:22-23: "But the fruit of the Spirit is love, joy, peace, patience, kindness, goodness, faithfulness, gentleness, self-control; *against such things there is no law*" (emphasis added). There is no law against the attributes of God that are gained through a loving and dependent relationship with Him. Joseph was not spoiled—he was favored. Do not let the devil steal your name and significance from your life. If we walk in the ways of Christ, we are favored by the Father as well.

Dreamer or Prophet

Joseph's brothers called him a dreamer (Gen. 37:19). They insulted him because Joseph shared two dreams that he had (Gen.

37:7-11). The dreams described what would take place in the future with Joseph's family bowing down to him in some form or capacity. His brothers mocked him and hated him even more because Joseph shared his dream (Gen. 37:5).

Joseph did indeed share his dreams, and they were prophetic. His brothers received Joseph's dream quite differently than what the dream was about. The brother's own feelings of envy and insignificance clouded Joseph's real meaning. "Though the dream was not ultimately about his siblings' humiliation but about their *salvation*, the brothers couldn't stand it" (Wright 2005, 103, emphasis added). Later in the story, Joseph was raised up in the land of Egypt, engineered a plan to prepare for the coming drought, and virtually saved Egypt from starvation as a result. His brothers and father actually bowed down before him, but the outcome was that they were saved during a worldwide drought. Joseph had dreams, but he was a prophet.

Being called a dreamer often has negative connotations. The dictionary defines dreamer as "an idealist" or "imaginative" or "impractical." However, having dreams is natural. We all dream while we sleep. Some dreams are clear and vivid while others cannot be remembered.

Not all connotations of being a dreamer need to be negative. Part of discovering our destiny and our purpose in life is to dream. Proverbs 16:9 says, "The mind of man plans his way, but the Lord directs his steps." Bringing our dreams and desires to the Lord is essential in seeing any dream fulfilled.

A prophet is defined as "one who speaks by divine inspiration and with moral insight." Being called a prophet may be an honorable label, but that is not always the case. John the Baptist prophetically called King Herod out for having an affair with his brother's wife, Herodias. Herodias did not take too kindly to John's revelation and wanted him dead. With a little manipulation from Herodias, Herod arrested and beheaded John (Mark 6:17-28).

Jesus often spoke prophetically, and He was mocked as a result. A prophet can help people feel encouraged and affirmed but also angry and uncomfortable simply because they share what God has said or what God has shown them. Jesus taught, "A prophet is not without honor except in his hometown and among his own relatives and in his own household" (Mark 6:4; see also Matt 13:57; Luke 4:24; and John 4:44). The Pharisees often ridiculed Jesus for His statements mainly because Jesus' life, authority and spiritual power threatened them.

Joseph was ridiculed and beaten by his family for his prophetic visions. Yet he remained faithful in his life conduct. Joseph may have had dreams, but he was more than just a dreamer. He heard from God and expressed what God showed him. I believe Joseph was able to withstand much of what came his way because he knew what he heard, what he saw, and what God said about him. Listen to the truth of what God has shown you, for He will make a way, and He will be vindicated. The truth *always* has a way rising to the top! It just may take time.

Overpowered or Overcomer

Joseph was overpowered by his brothers when they tried to kill him (Gen. 37:18-20). He was thrown into a pit without water and then sold as a slave to the Midianites (Gen. 37:24, 28). The Midianites then sold Joseph to Potiphar, who was the captain of the bodyguards of Pharaoh, the king of Egypt. Throughout this stage of Joseph's life he was mocked, abused, beaten, and sold as a slave twice. Even though he was favored by his father, Joseph could have named himself "victim," "powerless," "worthless," "damaged goods," or "undeserved." Yet several verses make it clear how he really stood:

- "The Lord was with Joseph, so he became a successful man" —Gen. 39:2
- "His master saw that the Lord was with him"—Gen. 39:3
- "So Joseph found favor in his sight"—Gen. 39:4
- "The Lord blessed the Egyptian's house on account of Joseph"—Gen. 39:5

Chances are Joseph became increasingly aware of the favor of God upon his life. As he continued to walk in integrity, he surely noticed the fruit of his heart. Eventually, Potiphar saw Joseph's integrity. Even though he was a slave, Potiphar placed Joseph in charge of his entire household and his wealth (Gen. 39:7).

However, when all was going well for Joseph, even while he was in a strange land, another curve was thrown his way. Potiphar's wife lusted after Joseph and wanted to have an affair with him (Gen. 39:7). He consistently refused her advances each time. She harassed and tempted him *every day* (Gen. 39:10). Can you imagine the powerful temptation he had to endure? Joseph knew his identity. He knew God was with him. He knew his significance. He knew if he succumbed to temptation he would be going against God. Read Joseph's response to temptation:

> But he refused and said to his master's wife, "Behold, with me here, my master does not concern himself with anything in the house, and he has put all that he owns in my charge. There is no one greater in this house than I, and he has withheld nothing from me except you, because you are his wife. How then could I do this great evil and sin against God?" (Gen. 39:8-9)

Joseph was able to withstand temptation because he knew who he was! He also knew God. It is interesting to consider the fact that Potiphar apparently trusted Joseph more than his own wife. For

Potiphar to not trust his wife with all of their possessions is very telling. Potiphar seemed to know integrity when he saw it. After all, his own wife went seeking after another man!

After being turned away time after time, Potiphar's wife took some drastic measures. She physically accosted Joseph, grabbed his garment, and tried to seduce him. Joseph ran, leaving a part of his garment in her hand as he fled (Gen. 39:11-12). Then, she essentially screamed "rape" and told her husband *her* version of what happened when he returned home. Potiphar believed her and quickly placed Joseph in jail, as a result of his wife's accusation (Gen. 39:19-20).

There is something very important about this story that is often overlooked. Let's look the passage in Genesis 39:11-18:

> Now it happened one day that he went into the house to do his work, and *none of the men of the household was there inside*. She caught him by his garment, saying, "Lie with me!" And he left his garment in her hand and fled, and went outside . . . she called to the men of her household and said to them, "See, he has brought in a Hebrew to us to make sport of us; he came in to me to lie with me, and I screamed. When he heard that I raised my voice and screamed, he left his garment beside me and fled and went outside." So *she left his garment beside her until his master came home*. Then she spoke to him with these words, "The Hebrew slave, whom you brought to us, came in to me to make sport of me; and as I raised my voice and screamed, he left his garment beside me and fled outside." (emphasis added)

When Potiphar's wife screamed and called out to "the men in her household," nothing happened. No one came to her rescue. No one arrested Joseph. Why? *Because no one was home!* She screamed but no one was there to hear it. This is a key to dealing with the accuser of the brethren, the devil. Satan desires to isolate us, making it easier for him to influence us. However, when he isolates someone, no one else is around to hear his accusations (not a very smart strategy). It is therefore important to know who you are in the face of false accusations.

The devil will constantly accuse and scream certain things about us. He will be in our ears. He will remind us of our past. He will try to tell us what our name is and who we are. But if it isn't true, it does not have to stick. Joseph was being accused of rape and infidelity. His integrity was being attacked. Yet Joseph remained true to his master, to his responsibility, and to his God (Gen. 39:8-9). He ran from evil! If there is no one home, if you will, there is no one there to hear any false accusations. We do not have to believe what is being said about us. The truth always has a way of rising to the top! Our name belongs to the one who knows us and loves us—the Almighty God!

Also, notice the drama of Potiphar's wife. When no one heard her screams of lies, she simply laid on her bed with Joseph's garment beside her until her husband returned home. She had to stage a scene so her story would be believed. Drama has become a big part of our society. Chances are if drama has to exist, then there are more lies than truth involved. Joseph did not want any part of drama. The Scriptures do not record that he even defended himself to Potiphar. Joseph did not add to the drama. He simply remained true to the truth, even if it meant prison.

Despite being falsely accused and suffering the consequences of actions that did not belong to him, Joseph remained faithful to the truth of who he was, and as a result, the truth of who he was rose to the top. Joseph may have been overwhelmed by mistreatment and falsehoods, but he became and remained an overcomer. He may have been initially overpowered by lies and false accusations, but he remained steadfast to the truth. He did not allow someone or circumstances to steal his significance. The truth of his name and identity was both given and confirmed by God over and over again.

Finally, even after Joseph found himself in prison as an innocent man, his identity remained consistent. He continued to walk in the identity his Father gave him.

- "But the Lord was with Joseph and extended kindness to him"—Gen. 39:21
- God "gave him favor in the sight of the chief jailor"—Gen. 39:21
- "The chief jailor committed to Joseph's charge all the prisoners who were in jail"—Gen. 39:22
- "The chief jailor did not supervise anything under Joseph's charge because the Lord was with him"—Gen. 39:23

Overlooked or Held Over

The story continues while Joseph is in jail. The palace cupbearer and the chief baker were thrown in jail, and Joseph was placed in charge of them while in jail (Gen. 40:1-4). One night, they both had dreams, which deeply disturbed them. Joseph invited them to share their dreams. He interpreted both dreams, and they came to pass just as he described (Gen. 40:9-22).

Joseph asked the cupbearer to remember him: "Keep me in mind when all goes well with you, and please do me a kindness by mentioning me to Pharaoh and get me out of this house" (Gen. 40:14). Even though the cupbearer was freed from jail and completely restored to his role with the Pharaoh, he forgot about Joseph (Gen. 40:20-23). So, despite his talents, Joseph became forgotten, neglected, and overlooked.

A full two years later, Pharaoh had a dream (Gen. 41:1) that greatly troubled him. He called upon his magicians for help, but not one of them could interpret it. It was at that time that the cupbearer remembered Joseph and his ability to interpret dreams (Gen. 41:10-13). Pharaoh called for Joseph, who was able to successfully interpret the dream. As a result, Pharaoh called Joseph wise, discerning, someone who had a "divine spirit," and placed him in charge of the project that had national and international importance (Gen. 41:38-41). There is no indication that Joseph conducted himself any differently even though he was overlooked while in prison. Joseph could have called himself neglected, forgotten, and overlooked. However, he simply was "held over," waiting for the Lord to orchestrate what turned out to be perfect timing.

The end of Joseph's story is important. His dream interpretations came true for Pharaoh and the nation of Egypt (Gen. 41:25-31). He was released from prison and placed second in command over the entire nation of Egypt (Gen. 41:40-43). Pharaoh was so impressed with Joseph's gifts and his God that the king gave Joseph a new name as result. Pharaoh called Joseph "Zaphenath-Paneah" which means "God speaks and He lives."

Pharaoh knew God through Joseph's life. Joseph's needs and longings were met in his relationship with God. Joseph's name and identity was in God. Because he trusted God for his true significance, Joseph experienced worldly significance as a reward. As a result, his life reflected God, for even the heathen to take notice. It is life for us to know how God sees us, and it is death to live by our own hurtful names and false identities.

His dreams as a boy also came true, as his father and his brothers bowed before him while he ruled in Egypt (Gen. 42:6, 43:28, 44:14). Finally, Joseph was restored to his brothers and father through forgiveness. Joseph's identity and dependence upon God was reflected in his famous statement, "You meant evil against me, but God meant it for good" (Gen. 50:20).

Because of his confidence in his identity in God, Joseph overcame

- Hatred and abuse
- Betrayal
- Temptation and impulses
- False accusations and lies
- Bondage and prison as an innocent man
- Mundane things of life (while a slave and in prison)
- Being ignored and overlooked

Joseph's life went from the pit, to the prison, to the palace! Joseph overcame to be ruler of Egypt. He became loved and respected throughout the nations. He never allowed evil done to him or his bad choices to define who he was. He remained steadfast to the truth of his life. His need for love, purpose, understanding, safety, belonging, and significance remained in God, and he was able to see great favor in his life as a result. Isaiah 62:2 perhaps is a fitting summary of Joseph's life: "The nations will see your righteousness, and all kings your glory; and you will be called by a new name which the mouth of the Lord will designate."

Despite what may have been done to you; despite what you may have done; despite what you believe to be true about your particular state; the truth is you are valued and significant to the Lord. He has rescued you and desires to give you a new identity.

Chapter 7
A Balanced Approach to the Self

*To everyone among you not to think more highly of himself
than he ought to think; but to think so as
to have sound judgment.*
—Romans 12:3

*Yet You, O Lord, are in our midst, and we
are called by Your name.*
—Isaiah 14:9

Perhaps I should take some time to clarify the discussion on significance and self-worth. In a culture where self-centeredness and arrogance is at an all-time high, the discussion about self-awareness and identity needs to be kept in perspective. The constant media attention given to actors and actresses, athletes, music personalities, and to a seemingly growing number of "reality" shows gives the perception that the last thing we need to do is build our self-awareness and self-worth. It is true that self-centered drama is prevalent in our society.

Unfortunately, self-centered drama is true in the church as well as in the secular world. Payne states:

> We live in a narcissistic age, one in which a sinful and blatant self-centeredness is the *in* thing and is being preached. Some who write on esteeming and loving oneself are confusing sinful and/or simplistic modes with healthy self-acceptance . . . it is only after we have accepted ourselves that we are free to loves others . . . when we hate the self, we in fact practice the presence of the old self; we are self-centered rather than God-centered (Payne 2001, 32-33).

To accept ourselves, we have to die to the old person and see ourselves as Jesus sees us. We need to die to our addictions and false self, and ask Jesus to resurrect a new self through His blood and forgiveness. However, we can only see ourselves as Jesus sees us by abiding in Christ and accepting His redeeming work in our life.

I find it amazing and sad how people become so easily offended over the smallest of offenses and inconveniences. I believe it is mainly because we are so unsure of our self-security and significance. If our self-security is perceived to be shaky, then we will react to what appears to be a threat when there may not be a threat at all. While apologies and repentance is important, we can become overly demanding of apologies. Sometimes, our desire for vengeance will demand not just apologies, but for the offender to grovel. As long as we hold onto offenses, we are imprisoned by our resentment. Resentment and a bitter heart will alter our identity.

It is also true that selfishness is a foundation for much of our behavior and many of the policies of our leaders, whether they be church, political, or marketplace leaders. Instead of encouraging integrity, humility, and honest and hard work as the standard for self-respect and contentment, our nation is increasingly encouraging a dependent "victim" and entitlement mentality. Our significance and identity are becoming defined by what we get and how we get it, instead of obtaining a renewed mind through the Giver Himself!

True significance does not mean our lives have to be broadcast for millions to take notice. True significance brings peace and satisfaction from within. Knowing we are valued, cherished, and loved are the foundations of resting in our identity. When such essentials are missing, human tendency is to go it alone and to seek aspects that bring self-love. After all, if we are not feeling it, we need to reach for it with our own ways. That worked well for Adam and Eve, didn't it? The eventual result is not peace, it is pride. Pride and ego are not the same thing. Ego is simply the sense of self. We can have a low ego or a high ego. Our ego can be damaged or it can be affirmed. Too high of an ego leads to pride.

True significance also does not mean that because we feel significant, we are entitled to our deep desires. To desire to have our longings met is not the same as entitlement. "The entitlement fallacy is based on this simple belief: because I want something very much, I ought to have it" (McKay, Rogers, and McKay 2003, 88). We as a culture are bogged down with our "rights" that we have forgotten that we live under privileges, not rights. Entitlements are equated with rights, and can be a false measurement of our significance. "The basic idea is that the degree of your need justifies the demand that someone else provide it" (McKay, Rogers, and McKay 2003, 88).

The truth is that by His goodness and love for us, God desired to redeem us and to meet our needs. We are blessed, not entitled, when He does so. It is His good pleasure to do so, and it is not what we deserve. "The entitlement fallacy confuses desire with obligation" (McKay, Rogers, and McKay 2003, 89). God is not obligated to do anything on our behalf. Our identity and significance is a byproduct of His love for us. Our surrender to the Lord's love brings us to wholeness, and a renewed relationship to God through Jesus. The good news is that God desires to fulfill and provide us with true significance in Him.

Scripture makes it clear that pride in oneself goes against God. James 4:6 says, "God is apposed to the proud but gives grace to the humble." Jeremiah 48:29-31 describes the pride of Moab as "arrogance" and "self-exaltation," and that his "idle boasts have accomplished nothing." Jesus' discourse on the sins of the Pharisees in Matthew 23:25 includes the indictment, "For you clean the outside of the cup and the dish, but inside they are full of robbery and self-indulgence." The apostle James writes,

> But if you have bitter jealousy and selfish ambition in your heart, do not be arrogant and so lie against the truth. This wisdom is not that which comes down from above, but is earthly, natural, demonic. For where jealousy and selfish ambition exist, there is disorder and every evil thing" (James 3:14-16).

Loving oneself to the point where pride, arrogance, and dysfunction occur is not the self-awareness I am discussing. Fenelon states, "Your self-love is terribly touchy . . . the only hope is to come out of yourself" (Fenelon 1992, 79). Fenelon adds, "We may be sure, then, that it is only the love of God that can make us come out of self" (Fenelon 1997, 37). Self-love can lead to arrogance. Healthy self-love can lead to self-acceptance and self-worth. But, healthy self-love begins with loving God and surrendering to Him.

When Jesus taught, "You shall love your neighbor as yourself" in Mark 12:31, He was referring to self-love. In actuality, the context of Jesus' teaching here was referring to three loves: loving God with all our being, loving self, and then loving others. Jesus was commanding us to love those around us, but with the assumption that we experienced God's love and that we loved ourselves as well. The truth is we cannot love someone else if we do not have a healthy love and acceptance of ourselves. We can only give that which we have.

Within marriages, self-love can be a hindrance as well. Ephesians 5:28-29 says, "So husbands ought also to love their own wives as their own bodies. He who loves his own wife loves himself." Once again, we can only give that which we have. I have often seen conflict with marriages escalate because of the insecurity of one or both parties, not just because of the actual disagreement. As long as we do not receive conflict and disagreement as a personal attack on our significance and identity, we will have a better chance of arriving at a resolution.

The reverse can be a hindrance as well. If we love ourselves too much, we cannot love others. When we are fixated selfishly on ourselves, we will have much difficulty noticing someone else. For example, Narcissus was a hunter in Greek mythology who, when he saw his reflection in the water, fell in love with himself. So much so that his fixation caused him to fall into the water and drown. We derive the term "narcissistic" from this character. Seeking after significance for our own significance's sake will get us in trouble and potentially destroy us.

Most of those we emulate are self-absorbed individuals. Artists, musicians, professional athletes, many businessmen and businesswomen, politicians, actors, and actresses are usually consumed with themselves and the things of the world. Many people, especially young people, want to be like them and experience significance in similar fashion. Many "stars" give the impression they are confident and sure of themselves. In actuality, the opposite is often true.

Self-absorbed people are hiding behind their success and find their significance in their possessions, performances, and accomplishments. When their life is peeled away, many are found to be quite shallow individuals. Fenelon writes, "The self-love, which is the source of your faults is also what hides your faults" (Fenelon 1992, 35).

What happens when they are no longer in the spotlight or no longer relevant? Often we discover that many of these stars become depressed and dysfunctional, since their significance is no longer what it was. Their significance was built on the sand of *appearance* and *accomplishments*, a couple of the idols of our day, instead of being built on the rock of self-knowledge and inner peace. Such idols fade and eventually lose their power. "The origin of our trouble is that we love ourselves with a blind passion that amounts to idolatry" (Fenelon 1997, 35).

Have you ever wondered why God hates idolatry so much? One reason is what we believe has power over us. Our beliefs have consequences. By our belief in something, we give it permission to give us our identity, which in turn effects our behavior.

The very first of the Ten Commandments is, "You shall have no other gods before me" (Exo. 20:3). He is making it clear that He is the One and only Creator and the One and only God. We are to worship Him and Him alone. This is not because God has an ego complex. It is because He loves us. "The first and most important thing you could ever know about a relationship with God is that He set His affection upon you before you ever contributed anything to Him" (Wright 2005, 97). The baptism of Jesus depicts this truth. Before Jesus began His ministry, before Jesus ever healed someone, before Jesus preached or performed any miracles, God the Father said, "This is my beloved Son, in whom I am well pleased" (Matt. 3:17). Jesus' significance to the Father was in who He was, not what

He did. We all need to hear the same declaration from our Father: "You are my beloved son/daughter, in whom I am well pleased!"

Essentially, man's attempts at self-sufficiency led to the creation of idols. "If we arrived on planet Earth self-sufficient, we would be robbed of the most developmental process of life—learning to trust that someone else is there for us" (Wright 2005, 97). God wants us to rely on Him. He loves us so much that He desires to bless us. Idolatry takes us away from the lover of our souls.

"The word *idolatry* can refer to the worship of other gods besides the true God, or the reverence of images" (Beale 2008, 17). Beale expands the definition of idols as, "whatever your heart clings to or relies on for ultimate security" (Beale 2008, 17). Idols do not have to be just stone or metal images. They can be whatever we pursue that helps to identify who we are. Our longings need to lead us to God, and our identity should be a result of our attachment to Him.

The Bible teaches that God is a jealous God (Exo. 20:5; Deut. 5:9; Josh. 24:19). Jealousy is not the same as envy. Envy is a sin. Jealousy says, "*I have something* I love, which is mine and may be threatened, hurt, or taken away, and I do not want to see that happen." Envy says, "*You have something* I want, and I desire to obtain it any way I can." The difference is ownership. Do you know why God hates sin? We belong to God. God hates the idea that sin and Satan can take us, and have taken us, away from relationship with Him. So the Father sent Jesus to redeem, or to make it possible to bring us back, in order to reestablish relationship with Him. God's jealousy is based on love, and He did not want to lose us to something other than His name and His image! We belong to Him. Our relationship was broken due to sin and Satan, and He bought us back. God deemed us significant enough to do a significant thing through the life, death, and resurrection of Jesus! I Peter 1:18-20 says, "Knowing that you were not redeemed with perishable things like silver or gold from your futile way of life inherited from your forefathers, but with precious blood, as of a lamb unblemished and spotless, the blood of Christ."

I believe there is another reason God hates idolatry. It is because He loves us too much to have us be *identified* with anyone or anything other than Himself! Human beings long to find identity and meaning. We often seek something or someone to provide identity and peace. However, as it relates to idols or to anything besides God, Scripture say, "Those who make them *will become like them*, everyone who trusts in them" (Psa. 115:8, emphasis added). Essentially, we become what we worship.

People take on the characteristics of whatever they emulate. "What people revere, they resemble, either for ruin or restoration" (Beale 2008, 16). Do you want worldly significance? Then choose worldly idols, which leads to ruin. Do you want true significance? Then choose Jesus Christ, forgiveness, and restoration. God's design is that human beings were created in His image, but unfortunately, people often instead become more like the images they create and pursue.

God created human beings to have, enjoy, and even produce life. God also created us to desire Him and worship Him. God doesn't just give life, He is life! Jesus said He is the Way, the Truth and the *Life* (John 14:6); that He is the bread of *Life* (John 6:48); and that He is the Resurrection and the *Life* (John 11:25). Pursuing God brings man to the ultimate source of life, identity, and purpose. In fact, "our yearning for God is the most important aspect of our humanity, our most precious treasure; it gives our existence meaning and direction" (May 1988, 92).

What most people do not realize is that what we yearn for cannot truly be met by the trappings and lies of the world. Our yearnings and longings can only be met ultimately through relationship with God. Lifeless idols of any kind do nothing to truly define who we are! Boyd states:

> The real issue is not what *kind* of idols people embrace but whether they are trying to fill the void in their souls with an idol at all. So long as people strive to get life from an idol of any sort, they block themselves off from their true source of life" (Boyd 2007,89).

I encourage you to change the names and images by which you define yourself, for they are manmade and therefore less than ideal, to say the least. Our emotional pain and hurts have a powerful way of defining who we are. Bring them to Jesus and give voice to our hurts and fears. There is power and release in the spoken word. Consult with a Christian counselor or pastor, meditate on God's Word, and sit in the presence of the Lord, for only He has your true name and significance.

Describing the sin of idolatry, the writer of the Psalms says, "Thus they exchanged their glory for the image of an ox that eats grass" (Psa. 106:20). It is amazing to observe what people have chosen to do to overcome pain and the lack of identity, outside of a relationship with Christ. It is equally amazing, on the other hand, to think that human beings were created with glory. Referring to mankind, the writer declares, "Yet You have made him a little lower than God, and You crowned him with glory and majesty!" (Psa. 8:5). It is clear that God has intended for human beings to be connected to Him, to reflect *His* glory, (not our own), and to be identified by His name, rather than to pursue idols and be relegated to eating grass!

We belong to the Creator. We are the children of the King. Very significant, if you ask me. Further discussions about idolatry will be found in the forthcoming book *Created for Purpose*.

Most of the individuals I deal with are not the types who are found during primetime television shows or on the silver screen. They are not usually the types of people who are full of themselves. They are professionals, the unemployed, pastors, military personnel, teenagers, abuse victims, husbands, and wives—all of whom have had to address the hurts that life often brings. Some situations are severe where deep self-hatred exists. Self-harm and self-abasement can be part a person's deep self-loathing.

Even though he was discussing toxic, harmful religious rituals, Paul made it clear that self-abasement and severe self-treatment were not things that pleased God (Col. 2:16-23). The individuals who I have the privilege of ministering to usually come to counseling because they know they are hurting; because they know they need help; because they know things in their life are not going well; because they are seeking wisdom and healing; because they desire more healthy behaviors; and because they need a healthy dose of the true "reality" that God loves them dearly and their life is significant to Him.

Individuals who make a determined effort to find out who they are, how to overcome the pains of life, and how and where they are going, usually find the answers they need for personal restoration. Once in a while I have had to deal with prideful and arrogant individuals, but the truth is they are hurting too. Denial, which is the failure to recognize our problem or predicament, is a powerful defense mechanism and needs to be transformed into confession. Remember, our core longings do not disappear. Our core longings are strong, determining forces that drive us to find who we are.

Essentially, we all need to have our core longings met, but only some people find true fulfillment in their search. Jesus can and does provide the healing and self-worth in the hurt individual, but the person needs to humbly confess his or her need in order for the Lord to restore what was lost.

A hurt person may not be hurting because of a sin he or she committed but maybe because sin was committed against the person. Many times it is a two-way street because we often make decisions based on our hurts rather than on hope. In any case, confessing the sin is essential for healing, redemption, and a renewed identity. Redemption is not just for our sins but for the effects of the sins of others. John the Baptist fittingly acknowledged that, "He must increase, but I must decrease" (John 3:30). Our brokenness and woundedness must decrease as well in order for our true self to emerge. Only the healing and redeeming power of Jesus can accomplish that. Whatever we were doing to obtain healing and fulfillment through our own efforts needs to be discarded and replaced with the pursuit of Christ.

In the teachings of the apostle Paul in Philippians 3:4-11, he made it clear that his standing among the community leaders, his zeal, and his accomplishments meant nothing to him compared to the "surpassing value of knowing Christ Jesus, my Lord" and "that I may know Him and the power of His resurrection and the fellowship of His suffering." The power of Christ's resurrection changed his life and set him on a new path.

The same power can do the same for people who acknowledge they need a Savior and a new identity. At the same time, he encouraged Christians to not think more highly of themselves than they ought and to have sound judgment in regard to self-awareness (Rom. 12:3). Paul did not say to not think highly of oneself—just not more highly than he or she ought. The devil has been pretty successful in leading us to either end of the "self" spectrum. We have considered ourselves worthless, neglected, and abused failures or we have considered ourselves as self-sufficient and arrogantly self-centered. In either case, the effect is the inability to have sound judgment regarding our true significance. The lack of sound judgment will result in bad decisions with harmful results. Other people will pick up on how we present ourselves. "When we reject ourselves or any part of ourselves, we communicate that view to others" (Payne 2001, 31). The sound judgment comes from a renewed mind through Christ and the awareness of how Jesus sees us!

Having sound judgment provides accurate perspectives of circumstances in our lives. Our significance depends on sound judgment. Despite what has occurred around or to us, we can still see things according to how God sees them. What we believe to be true usually wins out, even if what we believe is not true at all. Our significance usually hinges on whether we feel accepted. Unfortunately, we often seek acceptance through what we do, not because of who we are.

For example, we may say, "I am so stupid for doing that," instead of "That was not a smart thing to do." There is a subtle but huge difference. The first focuses on the self while the second focuses on the behavior. We all do stupid things in our lives, but that does not necessarily mean we are stupid. It is much easier to overcome how we feel about our behavior than how we feel about ourselves. God loves us for who are, and therefore we are significant. We love God because He first loved us. We can love ourselves in a healthy way when we first love God!

What we say to ourselves within ourselves has great power. Self-talk can be encouraging or detrimental. For example, in the face of several defeats, the army of Israel continued to rely on the Lord for strength and guidance. Their self-talk became important: "But the people, the men of Israel, encouraged themselves and arrayed for battle again" (Judg. 20:22). The army of Israel believed they could be victorious, and the rest of this biblical account describes a strategic judgment on the part of the army of Israel that led to their victory over their enemies.

Sound judgment can occur in the midst of pain, as long we depend upon God and allow Him to influence our self-talk. This was true of David in the Old Testament. In 1 Samuel 30, after David and his army returned to Ziklag, they discovered it burned and the Amalekites had captured their families. Verse 4 says they "lifted their voices and wept until there was no strength in them to weep." Have you felt like that? Have you ever been so discouraged that you have told yourself you could not go on? David and his men sure did. Even when David felt "greatly distressed . . . David encouraged himself in the Lord his God" (1 Sam. 30:6, KJV).

Self-talk can be a pathway back to significance, but self-talk can add to one's discouragement as well. There are several main types of negative self-talk that most individuals fall into: the *worrier*, who is prone to anxiety; the *critic*, who is constantly putting himself or herself down and promotes low self-esteem; the *victim*, who constantly feels helpless and hopeless and falls into depression; and the *perfectionist*, who never feels he or she will ever achieve or measure up and becomes burned out and stressed (Bourne 2005, 164-5). Any one of these will undermine our feelings of significance because they all are measured by circumstances and by other people. Many of us have given circumstances and other people the power to define us. Our significance can be restored through a right relationship with God, inner healing, and developing healthy relationships.

CHAPTER 8

Some Names We Call Ourselves

It will no longer be said to you, "Forsaken," Nor to your land will it any longer be said, "Desolate"; But you will be called, "My delight is in her" . . . for the Lord delights in you.
Isaiah 62:4

Albert Ellis (1913-2007) was an American psychologist who in 1955 developed Rational Emotive Behavior Therapy (REBT). He was considered by many to be the grandfather of cognitive-behavioral therapy, whose primary concept is that irrational and false beliefs on the part of the individual lead to emotional pain. For Ellis, active efforts to change the clients' self-defeating beliefs were the key to resolving problems and becoming healthy. Ellis believed it was the intellect that dominates our life. Despite being an atheist and a humanist himself, Ellis did acknowledge that belief in a loving God was psychologically healthy.

Albert Ellis's model does have some merit. After all, Proverbs 23:7 says, "For as he thinks within himself, so he is." He believed it was not the events or situations that affect us but our *beliefs* about what happened that affect us.

Ellis developed an "ABC" model as follows:

- A = Activating event
- B = Beliefs or thoughts about the event
- C = Consequences (emotions, thoughts, behaviors)

All three (emotions, thoughts, behaviors) influence the other; they are interrelated. Since the 1970s, counseling has mainly focused on cognitive-behavioral types of therapy. Backus and Chapian stated:

> Psychologists have spoken of "cognitive restructuring" or rational emotive psychotherapy or alterations of personal constructs. No matter which term the psychologists prefer, they are all excited about one major discovery, a fact that has long been known to wise men, including . . . the Scriptures: change a man's beliefs and you will change his feelings and behavior. (Backus & Chapian 2000, 27)

I would like to suggest that an added dimension be considered in Ellis's model: an activating event can indeed traumatize and upset an individual. The emotional and physical pain of such an event can be real. As a result, I believe emotional pain can often cause the irrational and false beliefs. A traumatic emotional event can cause a person to be "stuck" emotionally, often resulting in accompanying false and distorted beliefs. So, in other words, Ellis's "C" and "B" can be inverted at times. Wardle says, "Deep wounds are at the core of a several-layered cause-and-effect relationship between false beliefs, emotional upheaval, dysfunctional behaviors, and life situations. Christian people are not immune to this most serious dilemma" (Wardle 2004, 95).

As youngsters growing up, we receive many messages and "meta-messages" (messages within messages). Some of these messages are clear while others are underlying within our spirits. Each time we receive a message, it is engrained in our spirit and recorded in our brain, especially if there is an emotion attached to the memory. Abuse, molestation, and neglect often have meta-messages attached to the primary evil action. "God does not change the actual, factual nature of the evil which occurs . . . but God can change the meaning of it for your total life" (Seamands 1981, 136). History cannot be changed, but how history has affected us can be redeemed.

Another example would be when a parent tells a child, "You will never amount to anything!" These recordings seem to have a way of being played back throughout our lives in many different ways and circumstances. If they are positive messages, we usually live happy, successful, and fulfilled lives because positive messages breed confidence, grace, and peace. However, most of us play back many negative messages, or at least enough of them to often drown out and overwhelm the positive messages. If the negative messages rule the day, then a person often identifies with such messages and lives a fearful, unhappy, codependent, and destructive life. We are defined either by the experiences that often bring forth these messages or the messages themselves. Our identity has been altered when negativity and sin rule our lives.

In addition, when we are down, the devil likes to keep us down. He does not play fair and is a liar and deceiver. In fact, the Bible calls him the father of lies (John 8:44); the accuser (Rev. 12:10); and the one who blinds our minds (2 Cor. 4:4). As we discussed, Adam and Eve discovered from the very beginning how the devil will twist the truth. Satan will often find ways to perpetuate the negative thoughts and self-talk. He and his minions of demonic forces may be the perpetuating powers behind the playback of the negative messages in our lives. Backus says,

> Evil forces know our behaviors depends upon our choices, and we make our choices, to some extent, on the basis of what we believe to be true. For that reason, deception and distortion of fact appear to be the major weapons used by these demonic enemies . . . He apparently is able to insinuate thoughts directly into our minds. Such mental whisperings seem to have been his method of tempting Jesus. (Backus 1988, 25-26)

Rarely does Satan manifest himself clearly. His preference is to be hidden and very subtle in his attacks and harassments. The devil figures that if we remain stuck, immobilized, depressed, and wounded, we can fall short of our God-given name and destiny. As a result, we may become ineffective in God's kingdom. God desires to redeem and restore, so we can again regain our significance and identity. What Satan desires to use as acrimony, God intends to use as testimony!

Demonic influence can perpetuate false beliefs in an individual, and sometimes they can help a person justify an out-of-control emotion. When we hurt, the devil enjoys keeping us down. He enjoys adding to the hurt and keeping us deceived and confused. Satan will tempt us to self-medicate the pain and suggest that doing so will bring relief. Charles Kraft gives an excellent analogy regarding demonic influence, even upon Christians.

> Demons are like rats. If we find rats in our houses, we know we have to do something about the garbage that has attracted them. Inside a human being, emotional or spiritual garbage provides just such a congenial setting for demonic rats. Wherever such emotional or spiritual garbage exists, demonic rats seek and often find entrance. But if

we dispose of the garbage, the rats cannot remain strong and can be cast out easily. With people, as with homes, the solution to the rat problem is not only to chase away the rats but to dispose of the garbage. (Kraft 2002, 201)

The garbage is our false beliefs and woundedness and they can be "cleaned out" by the truth and healing provided by the Holy Spirit. The Lord's loving touch can heal, restore, and cleanse, resulting in the elimination of the garbage the "rats" feast upon. I am not referring to demonic possession. The devil does not have to possess us to be effective. Besides, a true believer in Jesus is already possessed by God's Holy Spirit, and Satan cannot cohabitate with God. The devil will tempt, he will powerfully suggest falsehoods and evil, he will influence us, he will harass us, and he will deceive us into thinking his ways and the ways of the world are better than God's way. He approached Adam and Eve similarly. Satan even tried to tempt and mislead Jesus, so to think we are exempt is naive. The devil looks for hurting and broken people in order to "devour" them in pain (1 Pet. 5:8). The truth, however, will always overcome deception and darkness.

There are countless playbacks of names we call ourselves in the recorder of our minds that have a powerful influence on our identities. These names almost always diminish our significance and who we are. Such self-talk almost always accompanies depression, anxiety, fear, rejection, and anger. It would be almost impossible to list them all here. However, I will attempt to provide some of the more common names and identities that we call ourselves. These names and statements need to be challenged against the truth and then changed. You may be able to identify with them, or by virtue of reading this list you may sense your own specific names that you have lived by until now.

Personal Confidence Labels

These following labels are some we call ourselves when we believe that we have nothing to offer or we feel helpless about our life.

- Unchangeable (I can't change who I am)
- Failure (I can't do anything right)
- Stupid
- Powerless/helpless
- Not enough/good for nothing/worthless
- Not competent/not capable
- Crippled
- Untalented

If we have low self-worth, we will be driven to always try to prove ourselves to others. Seamands states, "You cannot really unconditionally love others when you need to prove your own self-worth" (Seamands 1981, 72). The good news is that we can change, if we surrender to the Holy Spirit. Our lives are not hopeless. The Lord is more than enough for our lives! Every one of us has at least one gift or talent to offer. We can discover, enhance, and strengthen our gifts, and be released to use them. We may need to find someone who believes in us, and God can orchestrate that type of relationship.

Kevin Leman suggests some positive steps to take that will help. First, develop the spiritual side of your life (Leman 2006, 110). Find a church that teaches that redemption is possible for all who fall short. It is also important that holiness is part of redemptive teaching. We are not just saved *from* sin, we are saved *for* something! Know that God made you *and* loves you.

Second, use positive self-talk (Leman 2006, 110). Strict, positive-thinking only is not the ideal. Self-talk based on what God says is unshakable truth. Positive self-talk is an antidote to the natural human tendency to replay the recording in our minds of the negative labels and aspects of our lives. "Self-talk is usually so automatic and subtle that you don't notice it or the effects it has on you moods and feelings" (Bourne 2005, 163). The Bible states, "Finally, brethren, whatever is true, whatever is right, whatever is pure, whatever is lovely, whatever is of good repute, if there is any excellence and if there is anything worthy of praise, dwell on these things" (Phil. 4:8). Every one of us has *something* from the above scriptural list we can dwell on.

Finally, stop playing comparison games with your friends, neighbors, and others in your life (Leman 2006, 111). Our tendency is to place ourselves in the shadows of others, putting ourselves in a lesser light than them. We are *each* "fearfully and wonderfully made" (Psa. 139:14) and do not need to compare ourselves to others in order to determine our identity and significance.

For those who are disabled or handicapped, you are valuable and worthwhile and have something to offer in many different arenas. A person only has to consider individuals such as Helen Keller, Stevie Wonder, quadriplegic "mouth artist," vocalist, and author Joni Eareckson Tada, and American paralympic runner, Blake Leeper, to see how a person with limitations can still make an impact. Such individuals did not let their disability completely become their identity. Unfortunately, our society is not always encouraging enough to those who are disabled. We need to know that every life is valuable and significant.

Relationship Labels

The following are some of the common labels or concepts that we say to ourselves. They essentially lead to a driven behavior—that of keeping oneself from the feeling of rejection.

- Lonely
- Dirty
- Unlovable
- Unacceptable
- Sex equals love
- Only good for sex
- "Boys will be boys"
- I am a mistake

Among the typical activities that someone pursues to avoid rejection are spending time in isolation; watching many hours of television; playing video games for hours; viewing pornography; immersing oneself in exotic, romantic novels; and having sexual affairs. These pursuits have the illusion of "safe" relationships since, after all, there is no apparent rejection. One often chooses to be lonely because of the many labels above. God said it was not good for man to be alone (Gen. 2:18), but we sometimes believe it is not good to be in relationships. When we are separated from God, restlessness and loneliness draw us to seek fulfillment of God-given longings in destructive ways.

Being alone and being lonely are not the same. Loneliness is an emotional feeling that can lead us into bad relationships. Lonely people usually suffer from fear. The fear of abandonment and the fear of rejection are especially strong. The Bible says that "perfect love casts out fear" (1 John 4:18). Many people simply need to stop calling themselves lonely or hated and stop saying they have nothing to offer. Being alone simply means you are by yourself, and many times that can be a good, reenergizing experience. If a person is alone too long, loneliness often creeps in. That may be one reason God moved when He did to provide Eve for Adam. The truth is, we are never alone if we have a relationship with God. The truth is that

God's love "assigns you infinite value, eternal significance, and deep interest" (Backus 1988, 55).

Other individuals may have had love withheld from them or have been sexually or physically abused. Such people, women especially, can become vulnerable and "blood in the water" for sharks. They can become victims of continued abuse or manipulation that, at times, is presented as a form of "love."

On the other hand, it is not acceptable for boys or men to expect girls and women to give in to their sexual requests because of some male-oriented sexual or physical prowess. To give in to the "boys will be boys" mantra encourages an animalistic mindset. Men are more than a collection of drives and impulses—we are to carry ourselves with a man-after-God's-image mindset. Men, we can walk in self-control and respect for women. We are not animals—that is a wrong identity all by itself—we are spirit-beings in need of redemption. God desires to redeem us into our true significance.

Some common behaviors that result from low self-worth and withheld love are promiscuity or being in one relationship after another. Looking for "love" in all the wrong places, as Johnny Lee wrote in his song from the 1970s, can lead to undesirable and deadly outcomes. Self-loathing is a sure boundary breaker. We need to know we are valued and loved in healthy and honoring ways. As long as we stay locked in a victim mindset, we give the past the power to remain present in our lives. If we believe we are significant, then we will carry ourselves in dignity. Others will take notice and will often honor our boundaries. It is time to regain the significance of your life, place your life in Jesus' hands, and begin to see Him change your name into His name for you!

Religious Labels

Often certain religious names are sent our way from non-Christians and even church people who are not where they should be in relationship with Christ. Here are just a few:

- Religious freak
- Intolerant
- Weak
- "Holier than thou"

In one respect, the truth is that we are weak and all need a Savior. It is in His strength that we can live a faithful life and be effective in showing forth love and power of God. Philippians 4:13 states, "For I can do all things through Christ who strengthens me." Following after the ways of Jesus can place us in quite a contrast, especially in our world today. It does not take much to be different when holding onto righteousness and faithfulness. Standing up or speaking up for truth and righteousness is even more difficult today, since the repercussions often range from ridicule to threats of bodily harm. It has become more of a "sin" to be intolerant of a sin, than the sin itself. Do not allow the devil to discourage you and diminish your testimony. His intent is to wear us out and have us lose heart. Jesus said in John 15:18-19:

> If the world hates you, you know that it hated me before it hated you. If you were of the world, the world would love its own. Yet because you are not of the world, but I chose you out of this world, therefore the world hates you.

Hold on to your faith, commitment, and identity in Jesus. Do not let other people's mocks and ridicule determine your name in Christ.

Nothing can separate us from the love of God in Christ Jesus (Rom. 8:37-39).

On the other hand, may we not as believers in Jesus be arrogant or "holier than thou," as if it depends upon us to convict others of their sins. That role lies with God's Holy Spirit. The Holy Spirit has given us power, but it remains *His* power. The fear of the Lord is the beginning of both wisdom and knowledge (Pro. 1:7, 9:10). We are to reflect the Lord, not do His job.

Codependent Labels

Finally, if we attach our worth completely in the hands of another person, then we may believe the following names to be true of us.

- Perfectionist
- Codependent
- A pleaser/I must please everyone
- Acceptance addict/I must make sure others like me

The underlying lie to these labels is, in order to be happy I must be loved by everybody. Just *considering* such a proposition should wear us out! It is impossible to please everyone and be loved by everyone. We are to live our lives doing the best we can, with honest intentions, and with the understanding of grace. The contemporary writer and poet Maya Angelou made a statement that essentially said, "When you know better, you do better." She captures a freeing concept.

Hebrews 12:18 says, "If possible, so far as it depends on you, be at peace with all men." We can only do what we can do. Anything more puts us in a stressful lifestyle. Our identity is not based on *if* we are always successful in pleasing someone but as much as we are able, to give our service our best sincere effort. The Bible provides us with the idea that it is not always going to be possible. We may not enjoy having someone displeased with us, but in many such cases it may not be us that need the attitude adjustment. Do not fall to the other person's assessment of you, as if their comments defined you simply because your sincere attempts were not received.

These and many more often play back in the recesses of our minds. Often they are attached to our spirits and need Jesus' touch of healing and renewal. One of my favorite Scriptures is 2 Corinthians 10:4-5, which states:

> For the weapons of our warfare are not carnal but mighty in God for pulling down strongholds, casting down arguments and every high thing that exalts itself against the knowledge of God, bringing every thought captive to the obedience of Christ.

Take every thought captive. Consider it before believing it. Examine it against the truth of God. If it does not measure up to God's truth, intentions, and righteousness, then throw it out of your mind! Our beliefs have power over us. If we exalt a belief over the truth of God, it needs to be cast down. This process is part of our salvation—namely the renewing of the mind that Scripture teaches in Romans 12:2: "And do not be conformed to this world, but be transformed by the renewing of your mind, that you may prove what is that good and acceptable and perfect will of God." An unrenewed mind deals with the present based on our past. A renewed mind deals with the present, based on our future! The playback in our minds regarding our identity and names leaves us stuck in neutral and prevents us from experiencing the renewal God has in mind for us.

God still desires His children be fruitful and significant, but often we need a name change for that to occur. 2 Timothy 1:7 says, "For God has not given us a spirit of fear, but of power and of love and of a sound mind." After all, we are the King's kids!

Created for Significance

Look briefly at many of the individuals God used in biblical history. Their past may have influenced their lives, but it did not determine it! They may have had a past that was negatively significant, but God has the final say as to what makes someone significant. That is the impact of redemption. God made every one of these individuals significant by what *He* ultimately did in their lives:

- Noah got drunk
- Abraham was an idol worshipper; later he was also "too old"
- Isaac was a daydreamer
- Jacob was a liar
- Leah was ugly
- Joseph was abused
- Moses had a stuttering problem; he was also a murderer
- Gideon was afraid
- Samson was a womanizer
- Rahab was a prostitute
- Jeremiah and Timothy were too young
- David had an affair and was a murderer
- Elijah was depressed and suicidal
- Jonah was angry and ran from God
- Naomi was a widow
- Ruth was a migrant worker
- Job went bankrupt
- Peter denied Christ
- The disciples fell asleep while they were praying
- Martha worried about everything
- The Samaritan woman was divorced five times
- Mary Magdalene was promiscuous
- Zaccheus was too short
- Paul was too religious and a conspirator; he was also imprisoned
- Timothy had an ulcer
- Lazarus was dead!

No longer do you have to live by your old names and labels. Jesus has come to save you, heal you, and restore you to significance. If He can love and bring purpose to all the above individuals, He can surely do the same for you. It's time to have your significance be found in Jesus!

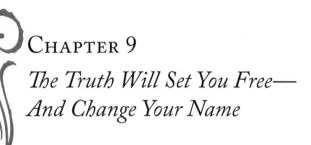

Chapter 9

The Truth Will Set You Free— And Change Your Name

Put on the new man who is renewed in knowledge according to the image of Him who created him.
—Colossians 3:10

Do not fear, for I have redeemed you; I have called you by name; you are mine!
—Isaiah 43:1

We have come to the point in this book where we need to discover or rediscover who we are. We may have been raised in a dysfunctional home. We may have been physically or sexually abused by a caregiver, neighbor, or loved one. We may have had an absentee father or mother. We may have been raised in a household filled with addictions. All of these and more can influence how we view ourselves, how we view our world, and how we view God. However, there is healing for you! There is salvation for you! There is a significant and new identity for you! God is your Father because He created you. God has given you a name and an identity.

We have learned to treat our relationships like we treat our "stuff". As a result, we see ourselves as "stuff". We deal with "stuff" as follows: we buy; we sell; we use; we throw away. That is often how we feel when we are in relationships. When our "usefulness" is exhausted (and who makes that assessment anyway?), we are set aside. In contrast, when we were broken, God still cherished us enough to give His only Son to die, so that we may be redeemed. He wanted us back, warts and all! We remain significant to God.

The truth is, you are a cherished individual who God loves and delights in. The truth is, Jesus Christ suffered and died for your sins and the sins committed against you, and He understands your plight. The truth is, Jesus Christ is your redeemer and Savior. The truth is, Jesus Christ has provided a way back to the Father. The truth is, He has called you by name and you belong to Him!

We need to allow the Lord to take off the grave clothes of death and provide a new wardrobe of a king's kid. The truth always has a way of emerging. The apostle Paul wrote, "For we can do nothing against the truth, but [only] for the truth" (2 Cor. 13:8).

"Are you putting me on?" is a common expression of disbelief and surprise. The apostle Paul describes a process of "putting off" the things of idolatry such as evil desire, immorality, anger, and abusive speech, and "putting on" the new self, which is being made in the image of our Creator (Col. 3:5-10). The foundational questions for the Christian are, "Who or what do I look like?" or "Where do I belong?" or "Who am I?" The *changing* of the life of a Christian to become more like Christ is the goal of the Christian faith. It is the ministry of the Holy Spirit. Being like Christ is what makes us significant!

There are several ways to discover and rediscover our identity. Since our identity begins with knowing we are created in God's image, here are several important actions to consider:

- Know your value in Christ
- Humbly confess sins
- Accept Jesus' finished work on the cross for your own life
- Know Jesus through relationship with Him
- Change negative and hurtful thought patterns
- Discover your new identity in Jesus
- Ask Jesus to heal your broken soul
- Forgiveness
- Break negative personal vows
- Break Soul-ties
- Grieve your losses and leave them with Jesus
- Experience God through His Word

Believing in Jesus is just a start. Our faith in Jesus brings us into eternal life. However, the Bible says, "You believe that God is one. You do well; the demons also believe and shudder. But are you willing to recognize, you foolish fellow, that faith without works is useless?" (James 2:19-20). I encourage you to allow Jesus to work within you, transform you, to "put off" the old names and labels, and "put on" the new identity that Jesus has for you. You are a cherished, valued, redeemed and significant individual.

Our faith is an *active* faith that, if sincere, will change our behavior and allow the Holy Spirit to conform us to look more like Christ. John the Baptist succinctly expresses the fundamental description of this process: "He must increase, but I must decrease" (John 3:30). As we discussed in an earlier chapter, the more we allow God to define who we are, the more connected and significant we become. Our identity and name are ultimately linked to our Creator. We become what we emulate and pursue. What is significant in our lives makes us significant in our own eyes and in the eyes of others. Instead of an idol, or an addiction, or the flesh, in order to be set free we need to emulate, or "put on," Christ.

There are certain things we can do to find who we are and be set free. First and foremost we need to acknowledge that we are sinners and have been sinned against. As a result, we need a Savior. Accepting Christ into our lives brings us more than eternal life; He sets the captives free from sin and pain! The Greek understanding of the word "salvation" (*soteria*) is really "deliverance into wholeness." Therefore, salvation is not just a one-time experience; it is an ongoing relationship with Jesus toward change. New thinking comes from the Holy Spirit working deep within a person. Wardle states, "Jesus always emphasized character transformation, a deep work of the Holy Spirit that brings lasting change at the very core of life. Jesus does not want people to behave. He wants them to be changed" (Wardle 2004, 76).

Behavior in and of itself *is* important, but it is not sustained without a Holy Spirit converted life. Benner adds, "Those who surrender obey. But not all who obey surrender. It is quite easy to obey God for the wrong reasons. What God desires is submission of our heart and will, not simply compliance in our behavior" (Benner 2003, 55). The sustaining power of right behavior comes as result of Jesus providing newness of life, a healed and transformed heart, and surrender to the Holy Spirit to be a changing power upon our thinking and behavior. God is our significance. Without Christ, we can do nothing. It is essential for us to live in His name, and not the contrived names of sin by which we have been driven.

We also need to change our thinking—how we view God, ourselves and the world around us. Cynicism and negative self-talk are prominent today. We are often told *what* to think in our situations and our lives, but not *how* to think. We get caught up in "group think". Social agendas, political agendas, and radical religious agendas seem to have the power to influence our thinking, even if it undermines our core values. Critical thinking skills are not encouraged. Instead of knowing what God says about situations, we go with the flow of what others think. The more I counsel with people, the more I recognize that we often ignore "red flags"; our own challenges to others' statements and beliefs; our own conscience; and our behaviors. I believe we need to honor our inner "still small voice" more often as it may be God speaking to us. There comes a time that we need to simply stop going against the truth. God values and cherishes His people, and he also values righteousness. Traumatic events may have happened to us that have affected our thinking, but God's truth about events and our life can overcome the lies we believe to be true.

Next, Jesus will lead us to identity and freedom through transformational inner healing. It is important to find a church that believes in the power of the Holy Spirit. The Holy Spirit brings forth healing and life to a hurting individual. Inner healing is simply a deeper form of being transformed into Christ-likeness. We may hear about the physical healings of God as He touches physical brokenness. The Holy Spirit is also interested in the brokenness of the human soul, and He desires to touch the deep areas in our lives that need restoration. God desires to heal our hurting souls and crushed spirits. Proverbs 18:14 says, "The spirit of a man can endure his sickness, but as for a broken spirit who can bear it?" Wardle suggests a six-step model that can lead to healing and gaining a new identity in Christ:

- Always take your pain to the Father.
- Tell God what happened to you, no holds barred.
- Open your heart up to grieve. You have permission to grieve.

- Listen to the life-giving, still, small voice of God.
- Forgive.
- Begin to walk in the new freedom and victory in Christ. (Wardle 2004, 101)

A large part of inner healing is forgiveness. We all need forgiveness, but we all need to forgive as well. Forgiveness is an act of the will, but it is also a process. Forgiveness releases us from several bondages: the bondage of sin; the bondage of regret; the bondage of resentment and the bondage of bitterness. I have included a declaration guide for forgiveness. Feel free to use it as a guide to express forgiveness toward an offender:

> I acknowledge the offenses and pain that _____ caused me. I acknowledge I have been deeply wounded by his or her words and actions toward me. While the offender may or may not have intended to hurt me, I acknowledge he or she may not have known what he or she was doing and how deeply those actions or words hurt me. I declare I am a child of the King, and the offender did not know who he or she was hurting. Therefore, I declare forgiveness to _____ for his or her words and actions. By the blood of Jesus and in Jesus' name, I declare and decree that I am free from this person's offenses. I now ask Jesus to cover me with His healing grace and set me free. In Jesus' name, I break the bondage of resentment and bitterness that has held me down. I declare that I am forgiven by the blood of Jesus. I am free from the grudges toward _____, and my life is now in Jesus' hands.

Another recommendation is to consider Christian counseling in order to be positioned for new ways of thinking and new outlooks on life. Most of us have altered our identities and significance because of various experiences and messages from our youth. Christian counseling can provide insight and antidotes to these false beliefs and a new beginning to who we are. Ultimately, our identity lies in Christ and how He sees us and feels toward us. The Bible says, "But we all, with unveiled face, beholding as in a mirror the glory of the Lord, are being transformed into the same image from glory to glory, just as from the Lord, the Spirit" (2 Cor. 3:18). It is time for Jesus to come and invade those areas of our lives that have incorrectly defined us. Bondage in our lives almost always brings "identity theft." These need to be broken.

We are also defined by who or what captures us. Remember the example of Helen of Troy? She was identified by her bondage. Are we "captured" by Satan and sin? Are we captured by traumatic pain and hurt? Or are we "captured" by our Lord Jesus, who intends to set us *free* and place us in right standing before the Father? The apostle Paul called himself the prisoner of Christ several times (Eph. 3:1; 2 Tim. 1:8; Philemon 1:1). In Ephesians 4:1 Paul says, "Therefore I, the prisoner of the Lord, implore you to walk in a manner worthy of the calling with which you have been called." I don't know about you, but I would rather be known by my "captivity" to Jesus than by "captivity" to any pain, sin, pride, or addiction. We must never be comfortable with sinful captivity. If there is an area of bondage in your life, and you are known by your "captivity," then confess it to Jesus, give it to Him, and ask Him to set you free! God's "captivity" is in reality the empowerment to be free in Him!

Someone who is in bondage to alcohol is often called an *alcoholic*. Someone who misuses drugs is called a *drug addict*, or a *pill popper*. These are just a few of many examples of being identified by something we are a slave to—just like idolatry! Successful substance abuse treatment centers are those that not just focus on the substance abuse itself, but more importantly on the underlying root issues and deep wounds that drive the addictions. The restoration of our significance in the Lord is essential in any recovery.

Vows

Some things that place us under bondage are obvious, like the ones I mentioned above. Others are more subtle and overlooked. One of the more diabolical ways we experience identity theft is through vows. I am not referring to promises that we make to be a person of our word. Nor am I referring to the "vows" a couple makes when they get married. The marriage vows are statements that represent a covenant that is being established by both the bride and the groom and is sanctified by God. Nor am I referring to the covenant God established through Jesus' death and resurrection that simply "vows" to promise eternal life to those of us who accept Christ and who "vow" to follow Him all the days of our lives. I am speaking of the vows we make to ourselves. Negative vows that we make from childhood through adulthood, that seem at first to be positive, are based on unpleasant experiences, unpleasant observations, and comparisons we make to other people or situations in life. Such vows bring us into bondage.

For example, if you ever said to yourself, "I will never be like my dad!" or "I will never be like my mom!," then you have made such a vow. Such a vow I call a "curse in reverse." I often hear these types of vows from individuals who come from dysfunctional homes or who have rebelled from their parents. These vows are carried through adulthood usually with industrial-strength power and determination. There are many such vows, and they bring bondage, not help.

The problem is two-fold. First, such a vow is being said as if we have the power to fulfill it. The truth is we do not possess such power. Only the power of the Holy Spirit can change or sustain a new life. Most of the time a person actually does become like their mom or dad, at least to the degree that he or she is unhappy with himself or herself. These vows can bring frustration and added determination within the person, placing him or her in a vicious cycle—the cycle of once again trying to fulfill the personal vow. Such a cycle becomes bondage. 2 Peter 1:3-4 says:

> His divine power has granted to us everything pertaining to life and godliness, through the true knowledge of Him who called us by His own glory and excellence. For by these He has granted to us His precious and magnificent promises, so that by them you may become partakers of the divine nature, having escaped the corruption that is in the world by lust."

Only God's power can change us according to His destiny for our lives. The Lord desires us to be who we were intended to be to reflect His glory and excellence.

The second problem is that living by a vow has us living by a promise to *not be like* someone. Rather, our energies should be spent seeking to discover who we are and living as who we are in our identity in Christ! We spend our energies trying to live a "not be like" life, rather than a "be like God sees me" life. We spend more energy trying not to fail than trying to succeed! This may be subtle, but it is critical in our false beliefs. Our vows to live a "not be like" life derails our significance. Such a life hampers our relationship with God and others. Jesus said:

> Again, you have heard that the ancients were told, 'You shall not make false vows, but shall fulfill your vows to the Lord.' But I say to you, make no oath at all, either by heaven, for it is the throne of God, or by the earth, for it is the footstool of His feet, or by Jerusalem, for it is the city of the great king. Nor shall you make an oath by your head, for *you cannot make one hair white or black*. But let your statement be, 'Yes, yes' or 'No, no'; anything beyond these is evil" (Matt. 5:33-37, emphasis added).

Notice that Jesus makes it clear that we cannot change something about ourselves, such as the color of our hair, simply because we made a vow. No matter what we vow to ourselves, we do not have the power to fulfill it in a sustaining way. Obedience does not necessarily lead to freedom. Freedom leads to obedience! We need the Holy Spirit to set us free and change us. He does so when we surrender to Christ. When we surrender to Christ we are called by His name, and our life will be transformed into who He called us to be. That is true freedom!

Ecclesiastes 5:5 says, "It is better that you should not vow than you should vow and not pay." So, below are the *basic steps* to deal with vows:

- Identify the vow you made.
- Renounce the vow you have made.
- Bring the vow before Jesus and ask that He break the bondage of the vow.
- Declare and decree that, under the blood of Jesus, the bondage of the vow has been broken.
- Finally, ask Jesus to provide the freedom from the vow and to reveal the newness of your life in Him, toward your destiny and true identity.

No longer do you need to live a life of "not being," but you can live the life of "being" through relationship with Jesus. The following confession and declaration is what I often suggest a person use to break the power of vows in someone's life. Feel free to use it as a guide:

> I confess and renounce the vow _____. In Jesus' name I break the bondage of this vow. In Jesus' name, I declare that my identity is not based upon trying to *not* be someone but rather to be who God had intended me to

be. I declare freedom to feel, to be real, and to be me. By the blood of Jesus and in Jesus' name, I declare and decree that I am free from this vow and that I am free to be who God intended me to be. Amen!

Soul Ties

Another form of potential bondage that often results in an altered identity is a "soul tie." Holmes defines it as follows:

> A soul tie occurs when the emotions, the mind, and the will of a person become entangled to the point where their thoughts are no longer their own and they are no longer able to function independent of someone else's thoughts (Holmes 2010, 10).

This spiritual dynamic can be known as codependency. In other words, someone else has been given the power to influence who you are and what you do. A person can "lose" himself or herself in another person, to the point where his or her own identity is overwhelmed by the other person. As a result, our significance is dictated by another person. Our identity and significance become linked to someone else. Our relationship with God is the primary relationship where we should allow Him to overwhelm us.

Also, our relationship with our spouse is a sanctioned and sanctified bond that God designed. There is no other relationship between two people that is described the way the Bible describes a man and a woman in marriage. They are describes as being "one." A parent/child is not described as being "one." Siblings are not described as being "one." Only a married couple can experience oneness. This soul tie is sanctioned by God, but no other!

Hebrews 13:4 says, "Marriage is to be held in honor among all, and the marriage bed is to be undefiled; for fornicators and adulterers

God will judge." If you are honest with yourself, you will be able to admit the regrets of promiscuity, realizing that something of yourself was given to another, and something from another was passed on to you. These need to be broken so your marriage cannot be defiled. Your identity and significance are at stake.

There are three basic types of soul ties: relational soul ties; allegiances, alliances, covenants; and sexual soul ties (Holmes 2010, 7). Good friends and healthy marriages are examples of positive soul ties. Being connected to someone who is mutually interested in you, as you are in them, can be beneficial. Jonathan and David had that type of bond (1 Sam. 18:1,3; 1 Sam. 20:17). However, God warned and commanded the people of Israel not to make treaties and agreements with their enemies and with ungodly nations (Deut. 7:1-2).

The apostle Paul admonished believers to be careful with whom they become aligned. We are warned not to make allegiances and covenants with individuals, groups, or organizations that are contrary to the principles of God. Fraternal organizations and secret societies are common examples of organizations to not make allegiances with. The apostle Paul writes:

> Do not be bound together with unbelievers; for what partnership have righteousness and lawlessness; or what fellowship has light with darkness? Or what harmony has Christ with Belial, or what has a believer in common with an unbeliever? Or what agreement has the temple of God with idols? For we are the temple of the living God" (2 Cor. 6:14-16).

Sexual soul ties are the most common and often most difficult to break. When two people become sexually and physically united, a soul tie is formed. Much more than a physical experience happens when two people engage in sex. I am convinced that two people experience an emotional, physical, and a spiritual dynamic when sex and intercourse take place. The soul tie remains even if the relationship is over. As a result, the behavioral pattern continues because a soul tie has become part of our identity and pulls on us. Often, we may know that casual sex is wrong, but we may feel powerless to draw the line because of own attempts to satisfy an inner core longing or for something we are bound to. Such ties need to be broken in order to get our life back and to experience healthy relationships.

Holmes suggests eight behavioral signs of a soul tie:

- Irrational thinking
- Evaluating the present based on previous circumstances
- Emotionally dead
- Fantasy attractions (substance addictions; romance novels; pornography)
- Unhealthy and unnatural desires and attractions to people, places, and things
- Lack of good discernment and judgment
- Inability to establish and maintain proper relationships
- Incapable of commitment to people or things (Holmes 2010, 27-31)

If you feel that any or several of these descriptions fit you, then perhaps a soul tie needs to be broken. After all, soul ties hamper who you are supposed to be and the freedom that comes in Christ.

Here are some *basic steps* to break soul ties and begin to flip the labels and restore your identity:

- You must want to be free.
- You must be willing to let go (thoughts, items, pictures, etc.).
- You must repent of your behaviors and contributions.
- You must renounce the soul ties (declare and decree).

- You must receive God's grace, love, forgiveness, and restoration (Holmes 2010, 49-51).

The following is a declaration that I use with individuals as a beginning point to eradicate soul ties. Feel free to use this as you begin to flip the labels of your life and have your identity returned to who you are to be in Jesus:

> I renounce and repent of my relationship with _____.
> I gave him or her my body and my soul. He or she gave me his or her body and soul as well. I declare and decree that I am no longer tied to _____. I declare and decree that by the blood of Jesus and in Jesus' powerful and healing Name, _____ is no longer part of my soul or my life. I declare and decree that I am now free to love my (future?) spouse without any soul ties hindering me from this moment forward. God states in Isaiah 43:1, "I have called you by name; you are mine!" Thank you, Jesus, for forgiving me and setting me free! Amen!

Lament or Grieve over Losses

This subject may seem a bit strange in our discussion of significance. However, the sense of loss is an underestimated aspect that can define us. We all have or will experience loss in our lifetimes. Loss is an inevitable part of the human experience, and grief is a natural response to loss. Death, divorce, and unemployment are common losses. However, there are many other loss experiences that can freeze us emotionally and redefine us. If a youngster is sexually abused, he or she often experiences the loss of feelings of security, wholeness, innocence, protection, and purity, to name a few.

Young people are not developmentally able to recognize that they need to grieve their losses, and many times carry unresolved grief into adulthood. "A child takes the loss of a parent, whether through death, divorce, or however, as a personal rejection. Unhealed rejections become seedbeds of diseased 'matter' such as bitterness, envy, rage, fear of rejection, and a sense of inferiority" (Payne 2001, 36). Victims of rape, physical abuse, and other trauma have similar issues. Part of the healing process is to grieve our losses in order to regain our personhood, identity, and significance once again. Psalm 34:18 assures us that, "The Lord is close to the brokenhearted and saves those who are crushed in spirit."

In 1969, Elizabeth Kubler-Ross presented what she called the five stages of grief. These stages may be more of a reaction to grief rather than stages since they do not always occur in the same order for all people. They are as follows:

- Denial and isolation
- Anger
- Bargaining
- Depression
- Acceptance

Kubler-Ross (1969) identified human emotional reactions to loss. To reiterate: we all experience loss throughout our lives to many varying degrees and it is natural for anyone to grieve when a loss is suffered. The reason I am including this prominent aspect of the human experience is that if we do not grieve, we often become "stuck" emotionally and mentally, rendering our identity as frozen. The reverse can be true as well. Sometimes a person can choose to be in constant "grief mode," also resulting in being stuck. This aspect can also become the grieving person's identity for everyone to see.

Everyone experiences grief and a sense of loss following the death of a loved one, losing a job, going through a divorce, etc., but the way these feelings are experienced and expressed differs across cultures.

In each culture, death is surrounded by mourning rituals and customs that help people grieve. Rituals offer people ways to express their grief and provide opportunities for community members to support those who are grieving. People adapt the beliefs and values of their culture to meet their own unique experiences, needs, and situations. As a result, grief responses within a culture vary from person to person, especially in societies made up of people from a variety of cultural backgrounds, such as in the United States.

There is not just one way to grieve. The length of time to mourn also varies individually. Grief is a transformational, multidimensional, and unique experience; no two people experience grief in exactly the same way (Knight, 2011). Yet in our society it often seems we do not have the permission to grieve, nor do we often give permission to others to grieve. We often feel compelled to hurry through the grieving process. The reason may be because grieving is believed to be a sign of weakness. We may be uncomfortable around those who grieve perhaps because we have trouble with expressed emotions. The truth is, grieving is not a sign of being weak—it is a sign of being human! The scope of this book is not to have a long dissertation on grieving, but suffice it to say grieving is a timely release of emotions that are linked to loss of any kind. In order to move forward, we often need to grieve what has been lost. You have permission to grieve!

The essential truth is that no one needs to be identified by his or her loss. Everyone suffers loss. If we were identified by our losses, we would all be carrying some depressing and debilitating names. For example, being a "widow" is a name based upon a loss. However, it does not have to completely identify who we are. It is important to grieve a loss. We need to know that we have permission to grieve and that we have a safe place to grieve. If that safe place to grieve is with a loved one, a pastor, a counselor, or a good friend, it is highly important that the grieving process takes its course. Allow grieving to be a release of loss and sadness, but also expect the Holy Spirit to restore and return your peace, contentment, joy, and equilibrium in order to regain your true identity. Remember, it is not what you do that makes you significant—it is who you are!

Finally, finding significance in our lives is the process of the Holy Spirit upon the life of a Christian. Accepting Christ not only brings us salvation and eternal life, it provides the process of change and restoration while we live on Earth. "Transformation is the process of undergoing a radical change of mind and heart, a dying to the false self and a continually assenting to one's true self, which reflects the image and likeness of God" (Moon and Benner 2004, 178). A true Christian is changing to be more Christ-like; to have more of the mind of Christ; and is in the process of wholeness.

Part of your learning journey requires your participation with the Holy Spirit in the renewing of your mind. The Greek term and concept of the mind is *nous*, which includes far more than your ability to cognitively think or memorize Scripture. The mind includes not only cognitions but also the ability to reason, to have perceptions, intuitions, imaginations, and more. Do not allow the negative experiences, names, and situations to define who you are. Put off your vows, addictions, and soul ties, and allow Jesus to heal your wounds and losses. You no longer need to be identified by them ever again! Your name is in Christ. You are identified by and through Him. "Man is free when his life is shaped according 'to the image of God,' that is, when he knows that he is living on the power of God, on the gift of God" (Brunner 1947, 170).

You are a sinner who needs a Savior, and you have been redeemed upon accepting Jesus into your life. Dying to the broken self is essential for the God-breathed self to emerge. "Self-crucifixion and self-surrender do not mean the downgrading of self" (Seamands 1981, 72). The Bible declares, "But you are a chosen race, a royal priesthood, a holy nation, a people for God's own possession, so that you may proclaim the excellencies of Him who has called you out of darkness into His marvelous light" (1 Pet. 2:9).

I encourage you to bring the darkness of hurtful, offensive, traumatic experiences and identity theft in your life into the light of Christ and His name for you! Peter, a broken man during his own life on Earth, wrote, "After you have suffered for a little while, the God of all grace, who called you to His eternal glory in Christ, will Himself perfect, confirm, strengthen and establish you" (1 Pet. 5:10).

If it helps, use this prayer as a guide, feeling free to add to it as you need to or see fit:

> Dear Father, I thank You for being here with me now. I ask You to fill me with Your love and peace. Please bring Your light into every dark place where fear, anger, rejection, shame, and despair have built up within me. Please touch me with Your healing power, and help me experience Your presence. Speak Your truth to me, chasing all destructive lies from my life. Empower me to live according to Your Word, Your promises, and Your grace. Help me to become aware of my significance in You and restore my identity. In Jesus' name, amen!

My prayer is that you find a new identity in Jesus. You are significant to the Lord! No longer let your name be that which has come from what others have said about or done to you or your own sin and shortcomings. No longer devalue yourself, the life you are living, or your future. Know that Jesus has given you a new name—His name—to live by.

- God formed you
- Sin deformed you
- Jesus reformed you
- The Holy Spirit transforms you

Meditate on God's Word such as Psalm 8, Psalm 139, and Isaiah 43 for example, and allow God to speak into your spirit, and you will feel encouraged. May God reverse your identity theft and bring significance back to who you were to be when He "fearfully and wonderfully" made you in His great Divine providence!

And the peace of God which surpasses all understanding, will guard your hearts and minds through Christ Jesus.
—Philippians 4:7

References

Anderson, Ray. 2000. *Self-Care: A Theology of Personal Empowerment and Healing.* Fuller Seminary Press. Pasadena, CA.

Backus, William and Marie Chapian. 2000. *Telling Yourself the Truth.* Bethany House Publishers. Minneapolis, MN.

Backus, William and Candace Backus. 1988. *Untwisting Twisted Relationships.* Bethany House Publishers. Minneapolis, MN.

Barth, Karl. 1981. *The Christian Life: Church Dogmatics IV, Lecture Fragments.* Geoffrey W. Bromiley, Trans. William B. Eerdmans Publishing Co. Grand Rapids, MI.

Beale, G. K. 2008. *We Become What We Worship.*: InterVarsity Press. Downers Grove, IL.

Belmonte, Kevin. 2011. *The Quotable Chesterton: The Wit and Wisdom of G. K. Chesterton.* Thomas Nelson Publishers. Nashville, TN.

Benner, David. 2003. *Surrender to Love.* InterVarsity Press. Downers Grove, IL.

Benner, David G. 2004. *The Gift of Being Yourself.* InterVarsity Press. Downers Grove, IL.

Bourne, Edmund J. 2005. *The Anxiety & Phobia Workbook*. New Harbinger Publications. Oakland, CA.

Boyd, Gregory A. 2007. *Repenting of Religion*. Baker Books. Grand Rapids, MI.

Brunner, Emil. 1947. *The Divine Imperative*. The Westminster Press. Philadelphia, PA.

Calvin, John. 1995. *Institutes of the Christian Religion, 1536 ed*. Trans. Ford Lewis Battle. Grand Rapids: Eerdmans, 15. Quoted in David Benner, *The Gift of Being Yourself*. InterVarsity Press, 2004. Downers Grove, IL.

Crabb, Larry. Editor: Tim Clinton. (2001). *"Knowing God."* The Bible for Hope: Caring for People God's Way. Thomas Nelson Publishing. Nashville, TN.

Cloud, Henry and John Townsend. 2001. *How People Grow*. Zondervan Publishers. Grand Rapids, MI.

Craig, Grace J. 1996. *Human Development*. Prentice Hall Publishers. Upper Saddle River, NJ.

Federal Bureau of Investigation. 2011. *2011 National Gang Threat Assessment—Emerging Trends*. http://www.fbi.gov/stats-services/publications/2011-national-gang-threat-assessment. Accessed March 27, 2013.

Fenelon, Francois. 1992. *The Seeking Heart*. SeedSowers Publishing. Jacksonville, FL.

_____. 1997. *Talking With God.* Paraclette Press. Brewster, MA.

Foss, Steve. 2012. *Satan's Dirty Little Secret.* Charisma House Publishers. Lake Mary, FL.

Foster, Joshua D. and Ilan Shrira. 2009. "The Narcissus in All of Us: The Occupation with the Highest Suicide Rate." *Psychology Today.* http://www.psychologytoday.com/blog/the-narcissus-in-all-us/200908/the-occupation-the-highest-suicide-rate. Accessed February 3, 2012.

Fout, Jason A., PhD. 2011. "The Sorcerer's Lordless Apprentice: The Powers and Political Powers in Barth, Yoder, and Wolterstorff." *Ashland Theological Journal,* Ashland Theological Seminary Publishing, 35-46. Ashland, OH.

Halley, Anne Medaglia. 2008. *Developmental Formational Prayer.* Doctor of Ministry course materials. Ashland Theological Seminary. Ashland, OH.

Holmes, Brian. 2010. *The Ties That Bind.* C4Promotions Publishers. Cedar Hill, TX.

_____. 2010. *The Ties That Bind: Study Guide.* C4Promotions Publishers. Cedar Hill, TX.

Kirwan, William T. 1984. *Biblical Concepts for Christian Counseling.* Baker Academic. Grand Rapids, MI.

Knight, Anita. 2011. *Grief and Loss.* eCounseling.com. Accessed March 26, 2013.

Kraft, Charles H. 2002. *Confronting Powerless Christianity*. Baker Book House. Grand Rapids, MI.

Kubler-Ross, Elizabeth. 1969. *On Death and Dying*. Scribner Publishers. New York, NY.

Laaser, Mark and Debra. 2008. *The Seven Desires of Every Heart*. Zondervan Publishing House. Grand Rapids, MI.

Leman, Kevin. 2006. *Pleasers*. Fleming H. Revell Publishers. Grand Rapids, MI.

May, Gerald G. 1988. *Addiction and Grace*. HarperCollins Publishers. New York, NY.

_____. 1992. *Care of Mind, Care of Spirit*. HarperCollins Publishers. New York, NY.

McGee, Robert S. 2003. *The Search for Significance*. Thomas Nelson Publishers. Nashville, TN.

McHenry, H.M (2009). "Human Evolution". in Michael Ruse & Joseph Travis. *Evolution: The First Four Billion Years*. Cambridge, Massachusetts: The Belknap Press of Harvard University Press. p. 265.

McKay, Matthew, Peter Rogers, and Judith McKay. 2003. *When Anger Hurts: Quieting the Storm Within*. New Harbinger Publications, Inc. Oakland, CA.

Moon, Gary W. and David G. Benner. 2004. *Spiritual Direction and the Care of Souls*. InterVarsity Press. Downers Grove, IL.

Olsen, David T. 2004. "Church Attendance in America is Declining." http://themoralcollapseofamerica.blogspot.com/2008/10/church-attendance-in—america-is.html. Accessed 12/31/11.

Ortberg, John. 2010. *The Me I Want To Be*. Zondervan Publishers. Grand Rapids, MI.

Overman, Christian. 1996. *Assumptions That Affect Our Lives*. Micah 6:8 Publishers. Chatsworth, CA.

Payne, Leanne. 2001. *Restoring the Christian Soul*. Baker Books. Grand Rapids, MI.

Pryde, Debi. 2009. *Glimpses of God Revealed through His Names*. Regular Baptist Press. Shaumburg, IL.

Seamands, David. 1981. *Healing for Damaged Emotions*. David C. Cook Publishers. Colorado Springs, CO.

Seamands, Stephen. 2003. *Wounds That Heal*. InterVarsity Press. Downers Grove, IL.

Stowell, Joseph M. 2003. "Who Is God? How We Perceive God Determines How Well We Relate To Him." *Moody Magazine*. March/April 2003. Chicago, IL.

Vine, W. E., Merrill F. Unger, and William White Jr. 1985. *Vine's Expository Dictionary of Biblical Words*. Thomas Nelson Publishers. Nashville, TN.

Wardle, Terry. 2001. *Healing Care, Healing Prayer.* Leafwood Publishers. Abilene, TX.

_____. 2002. *Healing Care Group Curriculum.* Ashland Theological Seminary Press. Ashland, OH.

_____. 2004. *Outrageous Love, Transforming Power.* Leafwood Publishers. Abilene, TX.

_____. 2005. *Wounded.* Leafwood Publishers. Abilene, TX.

Winston, John. 1926. *Fox's Book of Martyrs.* Zondervan Publishing House. Grand Rapids, MI.

Wright, Alan D. 2005. *Shame off You: Washing Away the Mud That Hides Our True Selves.* Multnomah Publishers. Sisters, OR.

About the Author

Christian counselor and minister Dr. Robert B. Shaw, Jr. is a Licensed Professional Counselor, dually licensed in Virginia and North Carolina, and is a National Board Certified Counselor. He is also an ordained minister, serving as a youth pastor, Christian education director, adult education director, musician, and executive pastor in churches in New Jersey, Colorado, Maryland, and currently in North Carolina, for over thirty-five years. He has also been a middle school and high school teacher and athletic coach in both the public and private school environments. Dr. Shaw has spent several years counseling in church settings and community agencies and with military personnel and their families (near Fort Bragg, NC) and specializes in trauma-related issues, addictions, victims of abuse, depression, anxiety disorders, life adjustment issues, loss and grief, counseling church leaders and pastors, and adolescents and adults. Dr. Shaw is a unique prophetic voice in the kingdom, caring for hurting people and serving as an adjunct professor for a Christian university, an author, and a conference speaker. Dr. Shaw has a bachelor's degree in religious studies from Wagner College, New York; a master of divinity degree from Christian International Theological School, Florida; a master of arts in professional counseling from Liberty University, Virginia; and a doctor of ministry degree in formational counseling, a practical theology, from Ashland Theological Seminary, Ohio; and is a member of the American Association of Christian

Counseling (AACC) and a National Board Certified Counselor (NBCC). Dr. Shaw and his wife, Lorinda, have been married since 1978, and have raised five children together. He is also enjoys running, sports, the beach, traveling, and spending time with family.

Made in the USA
Middletown, DE
10 February 2016